Religion and Art

Religion and Art

Rethinking Aesthetic and Auratic Experiences in 'Post-Secular' Times

Special Issue Editor

Davor Džalto

MDPI • Basel • Beijing • Wuhan • Barcelona • Belgrade

Special Issue Editor
Davor Džalto
The American University of Rome
Italy

Editorial Office
MDPI
St. Alban-Anlage 66
4052 Basel, Switzerland

This is a reprint of articles from the Special Issue published online in the open access journal *Religions* (ISSN 2077-1444) in 2019 (available at: https://www.mdpi.com/journal/religions/special_issues/ Religion_and_Art)

For citation purposes, cite each article independently as indicated on the article page online and as indicated below:

LastName, A.A.; LastName, B.B.; LastName, C.C. Article Title. *Journal Name* **Year**, *Article Number*, Page Range.

ISBN 978-3-03921-032-9 (Pbk)
ISBN 978-3-03921-033-6 (PDF)

Cover image courtesy of Davor Džalto.

Contents

About the Special Issue Editor

Davor Džalto is President of The Institute for the Study of Culture and Christianity, and Associate Professor of Art History and Religious Studies at The American University of Rome. He has published extensively in the domains of the theology of personhood, Orthodox Christian political philosophy, history and theory of modern and contemporary art, Orthodox Christian art, and iconography. He is also active as a visual artist, working in the media of painting, drawing, and objects/installations.

Preface to "Religion and Art"

Since the beginning of modernity, the relationship between art and religion has been a multifaceted one, characterized both by tensions and by productive exchanges. One can claim that the modern concept of "art" (and the corresponding modern institution of art) has been one of the "secular–religious" expressions of modernity. The language we have been employing to characterize the domain of "fine arts" and "esthetic" experiences has been remarkably "religious". We "meditate" in front of artworks; art allows us to experience a "spiritual" excitement; we make pilgrimages to see and venerate masterpieces in their (secular) sacred spaces (e.g., museums) that require a special decorum, inspiring the atmosphere of devotion. In this way (and following the lead provided by Walter Benjamin) we are witnessing an exchange between the "aura" of devotional (religious-esthetic) objects, and the "aura" of (secular–religious) artworks. This exchange of "auratic" experiences can also be seen in the exchange of roles between traditional sacred spaces (churches) and modern (secular–sacred) museums: modernity has turned museums into places of silent worship of sacred objects (artworks), while churches have become exhibition spaces where most of the visitors go to see artworks and not to celebrate the Eucharist. The most recent developments testify to yet another reversal. Increasingly busy museum spaces—with their ever-expanding use of technology and under constant pressure to embrace "participatory culture"—are becoming less and less of the old-fashioned quiet spaces with a focus on esthetic contemplation in front of a piece of art. Churches, on the contrary, are providing such a context for carrying out practices associated with the traditional role of the museum, outside the time of church services. All of this presents us with the need to reconsider the question of the relationship between art, religion, and the sacred. How can we think of the "aura" of (sacred) contexts and (sacred) works? How to think of individual and collective (esthetic–religious) experiences? What to make of the manipulative dimension of (religious and esthetic) "auratic" experiences? Is the work of art still capable of mediating the experience of the "sacred" and under what conditions? What is the significance of the "eschatological" dimension of both art and religion (the sense of "ending")? Can theology offer a way to reaffirm the creative capacities of the human being as something that characterizes the very condition of being human? This Special Issue aspires to contribute to the growing literature on contemporary art and religion, and to explore the new ways of thinking of art and the sacred (in their esthetic, ideological, and institutional dimensions) in the context of contemporary culture.

Davor Džalto
Special Issue Editor

Editorial

The Aesthetic Face of the Sacred

Davor Džalto [1,2]

[1]   The Institute for the Study of Culture and Christianity, 11000 Belgrade, Serbia; davordzalto@gmail.com
[2]   The American University of Rome, Via Pietro Roselli 2, 00153 Rome, Italy

Received: 22 April 2019; Accepted: 25 April 2019; Published: 1 May 2019

Scene 1:

You enter a church—let us say it is a traditional Orthodox Church setting—to attend a church service. Immediately, you find yourself immersed in a profoundly aesthetic environment, which evokes a variety of rich sensory experiences. You *smell* incense, the clouds of which fill the space of the church, infused alongside the scent of the burning wax from the candles. You *listen* to the chanting. You *see* richly decorated priestly vestments, in white, red, green, gold visually resonating with the colorful paintings—icons—on the iconostasis and on the walls. Toward the end of the service, if you are a believer and an active member of the Church, you *taste* the Eucharist—you *eat* the bread and wine—the flesh and blood of Christ.

To a believer, all of these sensations are pregnant with a religious, spiritual meaning. As a believer, you may even claim that you experience the *sacred*, that you actually *see* the invisible, *sense* the insensible. You may claim (following the belief of the Church) that you have (fore) *tasted* the sacred, that you have become *one* with the (eschatological) reality of the coming Kingdom of God. You realize that there is no exclusion between the *spiritual* (eschatological) and the *material* (historical), between the *visible* and the *invisible*, between the *sensory* and the *in-experienceable*, between the *thinkable* and the *unthinkable*. They become *mystically* (that is, in an *iconic* manner) united, without confusion. For a believer, the aesthetic dimension is capable of communicating something that does not (fully) exist in our world; aesthetic elements give a "foretaste" of the future Kingdom of God.

If you are a non-believer, however, all of these (spiritual-sensory) experiences in their phenomenal dimension remain "purely" *aesthetic* experiences no matter how intense or profound, no matter how sense-, imagination- and thought-provoking they may be.

Scene 2:

You enter one of the major churches in Rome, known for their artistic riches. If you are a believer, say one of the pilgrims, you probably experience the "sacredness" of the space upon stepping inside. The church, after all, houses many of the relics of Christian saints. Many important personalities and events from church history have been associated with this specific place. The paintings that decorate the apse, the nave, or the side chapels, the sculptures that depict religious scenes and personalities, *make sense* to you as part of the liturgical environment—as a way to help you immerse yourself more fully into the liturgical sacraments and the mystery of the divine–human communion.

On the other hand, to a non-believer, say a specialist interested in painting or architecture, or even just a tourist visiting the place for its important art, the site is primarily a place of *aesthetic* contemplation, pleasure, or just as an "attraction," which one should visit (and not necessarily *see*) when in Rome. Arguably, most of the visitors to the most *popular* churches in Rome go there just for that (pop) excitement, to be at an "important" place, and to take "selfies" next to the "masterpieces" as an important aspect of the whole ritual of this secular pilgrimage.

In this case, as in many other similar cases, the sacred space has become more of a gallery/museum space than a religious site. For most of the visitors, this kind of church environment exists to primarily house, protect and exhibit art (and other curiosities) for the sake of education and for enabling the aesthetic experience that these works provide to the incalculable masses of people coming to see them. Yes, there is the "aura" of the "sacred" that is attached to these spaces, but this aura is "sacred" primarily in terms of the "importance" of the place (in the cultural history of the West), its "oldness," the sense of tradition which these places inspire, together with their specific beauty (part of which are the visible historical layers of their decoration), rather than in terms of the religious rituals or some kind of the divine presence which is experienced there. The *sacred* is thus defined in secular terms, even replaced by the "secular sacred".

Another even more striking example of the way in which (formally speaking) sacred spaces can be understood and utilized by the majority of the visitors as *secular sacred* spaces can be found in the still unfinished episcopal cathedral of St. John the Divine in Manhattan. The "aura" of the "old" and "tradition" does not play an important role here (for obvious reasons), except through the formal references to "tradition" such as the (pseudo) gothic style in which the building has been built (which clearly differentiates it from the neighboring structures), and, arguably aspires to "borrow" a sense of the sacred understood (in some sense at least) as a *tradition-bearing* quality. It is a place which is regularly visited and admired by non-religious people for the riches of its cultural programs: exhibitions, performances, concerts (many of them very "progressive" in the techniques they use and the topics they address). The secular sacred seems to appear at the intersection of these *tradition-bearing* elements that shape the space and the contemporary aesthetic spectacles that happen inside of it.

Scene 3:

You enter a museum. Let it be a traditional museum of *fine arts* that houses numerous old and new *masterpieces*. From the very beginning, by the design of the building (many of these museums follow the traditional form of ancient Greek and Roman temples, even though they may incorporate new, contemporary, high-tech additions to the traditional layout), by the design of the rooms, and by the atmosphere of (sacred) silence and appreciation, you are reminded that the space you enter is a special one, different from other public places. The museum is there to allow the visitors to enjoy and appreciate the *works of art* (as some kind of secular sacred relics), to study them, to experience an aesthetic excitement by looking at them, and to meditate in front of them. This *setting apart* (from the ordinary context) of the museum space and artworks that are defined as *special* (i.e., masterpieces, aesthetic objects of great [aesthetic but also material] value) is one of the most common strategies of turning a place into a *sacred place*. Indeed, modern museums of fine arts have been conceptualized, designed and used as the places of the "secular sacred" worship. These spaces allow for the experience of the "sacred" but in "purely" (secularized) aesthetic terms. In that sense, they have, to a large extent, functioned as a substitution for the traditional sacred space (e.g., churches) that have also performed an aesthetic function, but within a (traditionally conceptualized) sacred environment.

This presents us with the difficulty of how to think the "sacred" and the "aesthetic" in the contemporary context. One can claim that the boundary between the two has never been very sharp, and that the modern attempt to offer an *enlightened* narrative about the aesthetic, which would effectively secularize the (traditional) aesthetic by turning it into a secular-religious (and, up to a point, civil-religious) phenomenon, has only led to an ever deeper confusion between the two, allowing for the many manifestations of the sacred in and via "purely" aesthetic means and even non-religious artworks. In all of the above listed examples, the boundary between a ("pure") aesthetic experience/pleasure and a religious/spiritual one is very blurred. Instead of "religious" and "aesthetic" experiences, we are rather confronted with a mix of various "religious-aesthetic" (or "aesthetic-religious") experiences that very much depend on our expectations and attitudes, such as: Do we enter a church as Christian believers, or as scholars who are interested in Christian iconography? Do we go there as art lovers who expect a (secular) "mystical" experience in front of an artwork (which may even result in the "Stendhal syndrome" kind of experiences), and do we enter a gallery to admire artworks that have already been introduced to us as "masterpieces," "unique" in their aesthetic achievements and their (secular) "aura"? All of these thoughts, expectations, convictions, beliefs, values and emotions (often diverse, even contradictory), determine our experiences of the ("purely") aesthetic and/or the "sacred."

In this modern "aura" surrounding the works of art (especially the "masterpieces") and in those modern spaces of "aesthetic contemplation" (e.g., museums), one can see typically modern (secular) appropriations of the (traditional) "sacred." Is it not the "aura" of something special, exclusive and valuable, what inspired the veneration of traditional relics (such as the bones of the saints), *cult objects as artworks* (e.g., miracle-making icons), and *artworks as cult(ic) objects* (the modern "masterpieces")?

Beyond the (unavoidable) ideological dimension which accompanies all aesthetics as well as sacred narratives, one can think about the significance of the basic elements of our sensuous perception for the character and quality of our aesthetic/sacred experiences. Modern art and modern scholarship on art have also attempted to go beyond focusing merely on the subject matter when analyzing the issue of the sacred in order to understand the relevancy of the very aesthetic elements of art and the artistic process (including the quality of the paint, texture, light and shading effects, etc.) for the mediation of the sacred or the very experience of it.

In some places, and in certain museums, people are still capable of "de-aestheticizing" paintings *qua* artworks in order to approach them primarily as paintings or sculptures with a religious significance and the aura of the sacred. When one, for instance, visits the Tretyakov Gallery in Moscow, one will not only find some of the greatest masterpieces of art history, nor will one only encounter the specialists, tourists and school tours there, one will additionally meet people who make the sign of the cross when they approach the icons exhibited there. These icons "radiate" their sacredness even within the museum/gallery environment, but one realizes that a "proper" way to *see* them would be inside the church (where, of course, most of them would be placed on the iconostasis, which means that in actual reality it would be much more difficult to *see* their entire surface and appreciate their visual elements).

It seems that the museum and the church have, up to a point, switched their roles over the period of modernity, up to the point that many churches in the West have effectively become museums and many museums serve as a substitution for the church in the type of experience they offer. It seems that we live in a time when both of these (secular) sacred spaces are going through yet another transformation and re-definition. Many churches and museums are embracing the "consumer-centered" approach and the all-penetrating "business logic." The kind of effects that this will have toward the type of both aesthetic and sacred experiences is slowly becoming discernable.

This all coincides with the rise of the "post-secular" era in which we are witnesses to a renewed interest in religion and the sacred in the West (which, one could claim, has never really been absent). We are becoming more and more aware of the complexity of the issues surrounding the religious and the sacred, as well as the ideological dimension and the potential for manipulation which is inherent to both the religious/sacred and the aesthetic. This special issue examines manifold facets of these phenomena by offering the reader six essays by eminent scholars working in the domains of religious studies, theology and philosophy.

In *Aesthetics, Music, and Meaning-Making*, Graham Ward presents us with his most recent reflections from the domain of theological aesthetics, which, together with the theology of the socio-political, remains one of his central theological and philosophical interests. In this essay, Ward explores a couple of fundamental aesthetic concepts—such sensory experience, rhythm, harmony, pleasure—based on Augustine. Ward dives into a complex analysis of particular concepts and their etymology, and the ways in which sensory phenomena come to *mean* something for us. This rewarding intellectual journey takes us, ultimately, into the realm of the created and the uncreated, where Augustine's understanding of music, and Ward's interpretation of it, situate aesthetic phenomena as indispensable aspects of our movement (in history) toward the eschaton—the movement in which the "meaningful and aesthetic are continually emerging."

Similar to Ward, Oleg Bychkov also inquires into some of the fundamental aesthetic categories and their conceptualization in the late Medieval period. *"He Who Sees Does Not Desire to Imagine": The Shifting Role of Art and Aesthetic Observation in Medieval Franciscan Theological Discourse in the*

Fourteenth Century is a philosophical investigation which is situated within the broader context of religious imagery and its meaning in the Western (post-*Libri Carolini*) tradition. Only when seen against this tradition does one realize the novelty of the approach of the Franciscan theologians in the fourteenth century, who came to pay more attention to sensory experiences (and the formal/aesthetic properties of artworks) rather than to the religious-symbolic meanings associated with images in the traditional theologies of icons. Focusing on the meaning of sensory experiences had another important implication: it required formulating a more general epistemology which would account for (tricky) sensory perception and experiences, but which would simultaneously preserve the ontic integrity of reality (as God's creation). In this sense, the question of aesthetics becomes linked with the question of the sacred (and the possibility of its experience) in the most immediate way.

In " ... *With a Book in Your Hands": A Reflection on Imaging, Reading, Space, and Female Agency*, Diane Apostolos-Cappadona offers the reader a fascinating journey, which brings together theological aesthetics and cultural history in order to unpack the phenomenon of visual depictions of women in the act of reading in the early modern Western tradition. Apostolos-Cappadona explores the social and cultural dimensions of the *meditative* and *engaged* act of reading a (religious) book, especially in the Protestant context, as evidenced in the art of painting. In particular, she focuses on Vermeer's depictions of the subject, all of which are as intriguing and seductive as they are visually appealing. What Apostolos-Cappadona manages to show in her essay is the convergence of the visually and text-mediated religious (and mystical) experiences of "theory" (contemplation) the (female) reader is engaged in (when reading a religious text) alongside a (religious/mystical) "practice" of reading and contemplation, which requires (especially for the purposes of visual representations) a specific *decorum*, specific pose, specific gestures.

In *Beyond Making and Unmaking: Re-Envisioning Sacred Art*, Daniel Gustafson investigates the relationship between Orthodox Christianity and modern and contemporary art. To this end, he explores a variety of classical as well as contemporary authors. What Gustafson's analysis makes apparent is the need for revisiting the question of the possibility of *sacred* modern and contemporary art (approaching the sacred from an Orthodox Christian theological perspective). This means that what Gustafson is proposing is an engagement with modern and contemporary artistic practices/methodologies and the sacred beyond the competencies of (theological) aesthetics traditionally understood. The goal is the actualization of the *sacred* as something that has to do with the very existential aspects of the human being, including freedom, love, and, ultimately, human eschatological existence. In this context, the (re)actualization of form and beauty reorients Christian art from its focus on "sacred" narratives (specific iconography) to beauty and the formal properties of the artwork, and thus suggests that we "should not expect Christian art [...] to strive for formal perfection, but perhaps rather to be elliptical, ecstatic, and epiphanic."

Both Gustafson and Randall K. Van Schepen, although in very different ways, explore in their essays the spiritual/mystical dimensions of materiality and aesthetic experiences in the context of contemporaneity and contemporary artistic approaches and techniques. Van Schepen's essay on *Contemporary Mysticism: Recovering Sensible Aesthetics in an Age of Digital Production* primarily explores the famous Walter Benjamin's argument on the aura and the reproducibility of images. He examines Benjamin's thesis with the help of a range of works by contemporary artists who use photography in a way which diverges from the visual properties of omnipresent digitally produced and digitally manipulated images. To the "hyper-real digital imagery" which "colonizes the material reality it points to, transforming our experience of materiality into one that is increasingly abstracted from the body," he contrasts the artistic practices that "mistify" (not a typo!) images "by occluding them in order to recover a more immediate and sensuous relation to the world, one that nevertheless also ushers in the spiritual." Through his detailed explanation of individual artistic strategies and technical/technological properties of their works (including their reproducibility), Van Schepen offers an important contribution to the broader discourse on the meaning of materiality (for us) vis-à-vis visual representations of the world, and the capacity of visual media to "re-materialize" our experience of both images and (mare) "reality."

James Romaine adds another dimension to the topic of contemporary art, its material qualities and its relationship with the invisible and the incomprehensible, with his *Beyond Belief: Chance, Authorship, and the Limits of Comprehension in Gerhard Richter's Strip*. Romaine focuses on the visual qualities of Richter's works (primarily his 2011 "Strip"), within the context of the artist's ambiguous relationship with the sacred/religious and the transcendental. As arguably one of the most prominent contemporary painters, Richter's art provides an important example of a contemporary artistic engagement with the domain of faith. To be able to believe in something "greater than ourselves," something "incomprehensible," appears, for Richer, as a distinctly human capacity. This profoundly human capacity is closely related to art, which appears as "the only means of realizing that belief in material and present form." Examining the technical aspects of the painting process, and the visual (and cognitive) aspects of Richter's works, Romaine also manages to rephrase the issue of authorship—which is, in many ways, crucial for the whole modern(ist) understanding of the artwork and its "aura"—relating it to the questions of (im)materiality and (in)comprehensibility.

In *Aesthetic Experience as a Spiritual Support of Homo Post-Secularis*, Viktor Bychkov explores the issue of post-secularity and the possible role of the aesthetic in bridging the secular and religious/sacred domains. With his status as a pre-eminent scholar in (Orthodox) Christian aesthetics in Russia, Bychkov's essay is also representative of a different approach and a different style of narration, which is informed by the great tradition of Russian religious philosophers and theologians. At times, in a provocative and even prophetic manner, relying on many prominent authors of the nineteenth and early twentieth centuries, Bychov discussed various phenomena such as *theurgy* and its connection with human creative capacities, and the "essence" of art. Bychkov uses the concepts of aesthetic and artistic "qualities" in an essentially Romanticist way. He contrasts those *essential* properties of "high art" to the "contemporary art practices" that, in his view, refuse the aesthetic as an important point of reference.

With that, I hope that the richness of methodological approaches and the diversity of the topics discussed in these essays will help us all unpack and better understand some of the most acute questions surrounding the use of artistic media and our experiences of the aesthetic and the sacred in our contemporary culture.

Funding: This research received no external funding.

Conflicts of Interest: The author declares no conflict of interest.

Essay

Aesthetics, Music, and Meaning-Making

Graham Ward

Faculty of Theology and Religion, University of Oxford, Oxford OX1 2JD, UK; graham.ward@theology.ox.ac.uk

Received: 13 February 2019; Accepted: 13 March 2019; Published: 21 March 2019

Abstract: The paper discusses the connection between rhythm and meaning based on Augustine's *De musica*. This central topic is illuminated by the analysis of other particular aesthetic concepts that one can find in Augustine (such as *sentience* and *desire*, in its many Latin variations), as well as in reference to modern aesthetics. The result is the emergence of a relationship between aesthetics and the making of meaning in a *co-creative* operation between the divine and the human based upon an understanding of rhythm.

Keywords: Augustine; rhythm; harmony; sentience; *ratio*

What I wish to present in this essay is a development of ideas found in Augustine's early treatise *De musica*, a treatise devoted to the nature and operation of rhythm. Working with, through and beyond Augustine, I will explore the connections he makes between rhythm and meaning that are developed theologically later (in Book VI of the treatise and then in his late work, *De trinitate*). It is the shift from the created to the uncreated, and how that is registered by or accommodated to our human nature as it has evolved that is foremost in what I am examining. What emerges is the relationship between aesthetics and the making of meaning in a co-creative[1] operation between the divine and the human based upon an understanding of rhythm.

The turn to the primordiality of rhythm is well documented in postmodern philosophy (Henry Lefebrve, Gilles Deleuze, Philip Lacoue-Labarthe, Julia Kristeva and, more recently, Giorgio Agamben, have each explored this terrain). It is well documented also in ancient sacred literatures. It has resurfaced as a significant theological category in the wake of a new translation and evaluation of the work of the German Catholic theologian, Erich Przywara (Przywara 2014), the publication of Raimon Panikkar's Gifford Lectures, *The Rhythm of Being* (Panikkar 2010), Michael Fishbane's *Sacred Attunement: A Jewish Theology* (Fishbane 2008) and Alexandra Eikelboom's *Rhythm: A Theological Category* (Eikelboom 2018). But I begin this present analysis with remarks from the Italian novelist and literary critic, Roberto Calasso. In his 2000 Weidenfeld lectures at Oxford (published as *Literature and the Gods* in 2001), Roberto Calasso asks a fundamental question: what is literature? In associating it with divinity, and tracing in the earlier lectures the appeal to the gods in early Romanticism through to Nietzsche and Mallarmé, he attempts to get beyond language well used and ordered in a particular literary form, to an underlying power and operation from which our very capacity to symbolize emerges and to which our syllables both express and inform. He takes this exploration back to one of the earliest of languages, Sanskrit, observing that *aksara* (which can be translated as an 'imperishable entity' or a 'syllabic sound', a phoneme) "is the irreducible vibration that precedes meaning, composes meaning, but is not absorbed into it (Calasso 2001)."

---

[1] On "created co-creation," see (Hefner 1993). For a more Christological reading of co-creativity, see (De Chardin 1964). My own reading of co-creation is much more in line with Chardin's (as I believe Augustine's is also). Maintaining the Christological focus is essential for avoiding a notion of "created co-creation" that too quickly assimilates divine creativity into human creativity—and forgets not only the infinitely qualitative difference between the divine and the human, but also how that infinite difference is rendered abyssal by sin. The Christological (and redemptive focus) stalls any conflation between "humanity's biocultural and eschatological futures" (Roberts 2015).

Calasso's attention to the primordiality of 'vibration' accords with one of the words Augustine frequently uses with respect to the theological relationship between creation and the divine: '*consonantia*'. Vibration at the origin of literature and consonance at the origin of theology opens a way not only to understanding the relationship between literature and theology, but it also enables us to understand a profound operation that is both aesthetic and theological in an encounter with what is meaningful. It recognizes human beings as tuning forks or viola strings—registering the meaningful as pneumatic and psychosomatic accordance with the rhythms of creation and relation and uncreated-yet-creative grace.

I'll begin with an account of sentience and desire as they attend to and embody any number of rhythms; then discuss the relationship between movement and reason, and explain why Augustine (despite translators) does not use the word 'harmony'; and conclude with the consequences of this analysis for a theological approach to not meaning as such but what is meaningful. I'll also explain why the conceptual abstraction of 'meaning' is not as helpful, theologically, as the adverbial and adjectival use of 'meaningful'.

1. Sentience and Desire

In Ancient Greek, αἴσθησισ is 'sensation' or 'perception', so what we are treating here in the relationship between rhythmic vibration, aesthetics, and meaning is sentience itself and how we creatively *make* sense of it. Nothing can be meaningful to us without sentience and sentience is many-layered. As human agents, we are consciously governed not by what we sense—the manifold of this would overwhelm us—but rather by what we attend to in what we sense. Our bodies are continually extending into the world around us, both passively receiving what is given and actively reaching out—for light, for air, for warmth, for food, etc. Mental awareness is limited; consciousness of what is most well-lit in the frontal cortex in these myriad exchanges, relays, feeding, and feedback systems. Much is taken in that which is not processed, while nevertheless impressing itself upon us and triggering responses that are autonomic and unconscious. But we 'attend' to somethings rather than others, and in the selectiveness of that attentiveness we accord value and significance. What is valued and significant can vary in intensity depending upon circumstance; vary in relevance to those circumstances. That doesn't mean that the making of meaning is arbitrary because everything is in flux and we construct what regularities there might be and build our lives around and upon them. Neither does it mean that the meaningful is all relative to the embodied intelligence *making* the sense (and so fall foul to some version of the anthropic principle[2]. It means that we *make* sense as some consonance emerges between *how* we process the world internally and *what* our experience of the world gives us. Some relationship between sonance and resonance, rhythm and vibration, establishes the meaningful. 'Con-sonance' is to 'sound *together*'. The meaning made isn't simply 'out there' as some outlying entity nor our mental construction.

In fact, meaning is not an object at all. It lies in what Kierkegaard, describing truth, called "an approximation-process" (Kierkegaard 1941) issuing from every relationship made and encountered; every connection and association given, responded to and surrendered. The sentient world becomes meaningful in and through the threads of these concordant relations.

There is a question about that 'attending to'. We can intellectually attend to and abstract from and move towards various orders of representation. But beneath that mindful focusing and forensic sifting much must remain inchoate. That is, registered at the level of the somatic and affective. The selection of what we attend to we might understand as an act of will, but the realm I'm trying to explore between

---

[2] There are 'weak' and 'strong' versions of the anthropic principle which explicitly addresses the correspondence between the human mind and the order we see in the world. The basic question is whether the order is out there and external or that, through adaptation, human beings have evolved to perceive order. If the order is in the universe itself, then a question arises about whether this order is indicative of a divine 'design' or a self-organization principle inherent to matter itself. See (Barrow and Tipler 1986).

sentience and meaning, sonance and consonance, is prior to self in any defined determinations of an ego. We might call this an operation of a proto-self, for there is agency, but not a definitive agent as such (Damasio 2000). The body has its own autonomic regulations beneath consciousness. It makes selections that we process much further downstream. There are levels of memory too which function involuntarily; body memory, genetic and epigenetic memory handed down to us as a species. There are levels of affect that operate through neurotransmissions, endocrinal discharges, and ionized-chemical catalysts through which moods are stirred and atmospheres are intuited. The intuited is felt rather than thought; felt valences that activate connections to low representational states. The shift here is between the instinctive and visceral and what the poet John Keats, in describing the poetic imagination, called "half-knowledge" (Gittings 1970); the lunar subconscious world out of which dreaming and imagining emerge. Our attentiveness and responsiveness is not a determination of any hard-core self; any conceptions of the self are arrived at, and change over time and under the pressure of different circumstances. Our conceptions of self (often narrativized) emerge through these deeper and unconscious determinations that attend to what is salient in the environments we encounter[3]. Attentiveness, not conscious willing, drives the aesthetic process.

For Augustine—remarkably in agreement with contemporary neuroscience—attentiveness is driven by desire. The word he uses and often gets translated as 'will' is *voluntas*, but '*voluntas*' is a wanting and a wishing that ultimately has no object other than God (who is not an object). Desire attaches itself to any number of objects in the world; but for Augustine, beyond physical needs like hunger and thirst, these objects are all displacements: things we think we desire when we are desiring. In this way, desire acquires many faces depending upon what it attaches itself to. It gains many names. In *Confessions*, desire circulates through a number of verbs, nouns, adjectives, and adverbs (*voleo* and *voluntatis, amo* and *amicitia, fornicatio* and *adultero, affectione* and *affectus, petendus, optatio, cupio,* and *cupiditas, voluptatis, diligio, delectione,* and *dulcissimus, libido* and *stuprum,* and *incundus*).

Recent cognitive scientists exploring emotional life observe that emotions of whatever kind heighten awareness and signify the need to attend to something even prior to appraisal. Emotions initiate the appraising. This attentiveness that emotions alert us have been termed "relevance detectors" and they have an "action tendency" (Phelps 2006; Frijda 2008). But Augustine's anthropology is theological, and so underwritten by a sense that meaning is not just made in and through all our interactions with the created world. Meaning is always given in, through, and beyond that world—making creation and our engagement with it *meaningful*. There is, then, ultimately something missing in what we encounter in our mundane environments. And we are aware it is missing, so we are nomadic creatures propelled beyond ourselves by a sense that we are incomplete; that the *meaningful* intimates a meaning that eludes us. Hence, we are governed by a longing to "know even as we are known"—as St. Paul puts it in his *First Letter to the Corinthians* (I Cor.13.12).

A teleonomy informs what Augustine considers basic to consonance, and that is movement[4]. I say teleonomy rather than teleology[5]. There is, of course, a teleology of desire in Augustine: he accepts theologically that, being made in the image of God, human beings are intrinsically created in such a

---

[3] Evolutionary psychologists would view such 'salience' in terms of pleasure and pain, biological reward and biological defense against threat. For an evolutionary psychologist's approach to aesthetics, see (Chatterjee 2014). Despite the neurological insights in how art (mainly painting) interacts with the various operations of the brain, it is difficult to avoid the sense that such 'appreciation' reduces the aesthetic to evolutionary functionalism.

[4] On the primordiality of movement and its association with life, see Book I of Augustine's *De musica* and, more recently (without a number of references to Aristotle but not to Augustine), (Sheets-Johnstone 2011).

[5] 'Teleonomy' is the recognition in evolutionary biology that organisms develop in accord with a certain directedness and purpose, even though overall evolution itself is random and accident-driven. Terrence W. Deacon succinctly sums up both what is meant by the term and the question it poses to biology: "natural selection is indeed a thoroughly non-teleological process. Yet the specific organic properties which this account ignores, and on which it depends, are inextricably bound up with teleological concepts, such as adaptation, function, information, and so forth" (Deacon 2012). Teleonomy is, therefore, some form of "unguided 'design'" (p. 124). All teleonomy involves movement through time, contingent circumstance, and complex forms of circular causality—there would be no "adaptation, function, information, and so forth" otherwise.

way that they find themselves, their human meaning, in Christ who *is* the image and likeness of God. But the teleonomy structures physiological and psychological (inseparable aspects of being human for Augustine) movement as the *anima* (soul or mind) is both animated and animates. The directedness of this organic structuring that forms the human person and governs the shape of individual biographies is, in itself, blind. The human person cannot grasp their own destiny just as they cannot grasp the providential care of God. They are caught up in a directedness that sometimes may be illuminated for them, by God, but otherwise is a following and discipleship of utter trust and dependency. Of course, a human person can determine a direction and a purpose for themselves, and *forge* their own destinies. But, for Augustine, this would be an act of *libido dominandi* and is sinful insofar as it fails to listen well and be obedient to the true and meaningful movement and rhythms working within and upon them. The verbs to hear and to obey are closely associated in the Biblical languages. Such a determinative *forging* would constitute a life of dissonance. It would therefore lack meaning. It would draw itself back towards the nothingness from which creation emerged, the formlessness over which the Spirit *moved*. It is the Spirit (of life) that animates and ensouls. The Latin word Augustine frequently uses for these ego-imposed determinations is *inanis* (what is deprived of meaning, formless, futile). The word is used in the Latin Bible for that which existed prior to creation when "*terra autem erat inanis et vacua*" (Gen.1.1). All aesthetic activity is related to making sense of what is sensed.

2. Movement and Reason

Desire, then, for Augustine, is more like 'life-principle', what Spinoza called *conatus* and Kant the "feeling of life." Translated outside the field of the philosophers and transposed into evolutionary psychology, we might find parallels here with Panksepp's 'seeking' instinct (Panksepp 1998) and Berridge's 'wanting' instinct[6]. It operates compulsively at a bioenergetic level (need for food and water; the needs of the metabolism), a physiological and affective level, a psychological and spiritual level, and a sociological and political level. It is that which 'moves', and in *De musica* Augustine will not distinguish between any metaphorical, analogical, or kinetic differences in such movement. Emotion and movement are both *motus* in Latin. To move is to feel (in both its sensory and affective registers); to feel forwards in accordance with a basic hedonic (pleasure/pain) scale. Movement is a groping in which the meaningful gets composed; it installs a directedness towards what will become meaningful. As we move or are moved, we *make* sense because we are projected into a world that enfolds us and are required by our proprioceptive senses to orient ourselves *in relation to*. There can be no engagement with the world without this corporeal and sensory orientation. That becomes the basis, not just for self-awareness (without which there can be no experience of what is being experienced), but an evaluation (not necessarily intellectual or aesthetic, it could be instinctual) of what relations are salient, and what relations the body in its orientation simply ignores. What is salient may be, at first, those relations that are most beneficial or rewarding (pleasurable). Meaning-making is beneficial because it composes us at cognitive and physiological levels; the more our environment challenges our sense to make our experience of it meaningful, the more we become anxious. So, what is salient can also include those relations that are unfamiliar and evoke curiosity and the need to understand. Movement projects us then into dissonances and consonances triggering, at the neurological level (prior to will-lit cognition, but feeding into it), comparisons, contrasts, integrations, and competitions.

Movement primes expectations in the *making* of sense. If it encounters the familiar, it also encounters the surprising. So, movement discovers. But it is not what is discovered that is most important. What is most important is the discovering, because it is that which lies the forging of new relations. Movement is dynamic, which means knowledge of the world is always temporary, always open to reassessment and recalibration. And the knowledge is not composed at the level of cognition and reason (*ratio*), but more primordially where what is inner and instinctive encounters

---

[6] (Berridge 1996). For a review of both Panksepp and Berridge on instinctive drives, see (Ellis and Solms 2017).

what is intuited through the movement outwards. So, we have three states here: the instinctive and 'hard-wired' internal response, the propulsion outwards, and the intuited relation between the internal and the external. Both instincts and propulsion are felt conditions—*e-motions*. The meaningful *made* in and as the relations is always incomplete and so always searching for greater understanding; though a certain resolution between the dissonances and the consonances is afforded in the emergence of patterns and regularities in which the inner and the outer animate each other. Such patterning and regulation are intimations of the rhythmic written in creation, for Augustine. Hence Book VI of *De musica* bears the rhythm of prosodic meter discussed in the other five books towards a theology of creation and a cosmology. Creation hums and vibrates and human beings are enfolded in such concordance, resonating with it. I will say more about reasoning (*ratio*) later, but at this point I will observe that, throughout *De musica*, Augustine plays with the Latin *ratio* as both reason and proportionality (the Greek *analogia*), and proportionality is the measure of and in movement.

The relations between inner and outer that emerge in movement are not always predictable; the new ones arrive as the unexpected. Learning, understanding, and artistic fabrications all issue from an exchange of energies between the internal and the external: the feeding, consumption, and propulsion that movement installs in all living things. The cycles of these exchanges, which correlate the various internal rhythms of the organism with the external rhythms of the environment, compose the creativity (and expenditure) involved in meaning-making. There is no necessity here in the forging of these relations; no determinism. The meaningful emerges in and through the animations over formlessness. Theologically speaking, meaning-making is an *imitatio* of creation *ex nihilo*; and ultimately, for Augustine, an *imitatio Christi* through whom creation came to be. As creatures who also create—where creation can be aesthetic production, technological advancement, or craftsmanship—our 'creations' are of a secondary, derivative order[7]. For creatures, the continual and dynamic emergence of the meaningful as propelled by movement itself is always striving towards a vanishing point—where expectation comes to rest. So, theologically read, something eschatological adheres to all animation as animation impels expectation. Something eschatological adheres also to all our 'creations' even the most disturbing and apocalyptic[8].

3. Avoiding Harmony: The Theological Difference

It is here we might think through three central threads in Augustine's analysis in *De musica*[9], each of which is not without theological corollaries. The first is *the difference* movement installs. The second is that play in Latin on the term *ratio*. The third is why, despite several English translators, Augustine examination of the play of rhythms in which human living and responding is situated with respect to the operations of the divine avoids the term 'harmony'.

De musica opens with the teacher instructing his student in how to listen to a fundamental difference. The fundamental difference he has in mind, and which is constitutive of movement, is in the slack and stress beats within poetry. They start with the simplest rhythmic movements, in prosody called 'feet' (*podus*) of the dactyl (stress/slack) and the iambic (slack/stress). There is, and poets, composers, and dancers have all pointed to this, a genuine association between ambulation and rhythm: *podus* is an anatomical foot as much as a term in prosody. I'm not sure the term 'metaphor' holds here;

---

[7] J.R. Tolkien understood this activity as "sub-creation." See his essay (Tolkien 2008).

[8] This eschatology can be more or less expressive. Broadly speaking, because technology serves not just the pragmatics of the present situation, but its own future advancement then the scientific imagination dreams of either dystopias or utopias. It draws material for either of these scenarios from what is at hand in the culture, drawing significantly on religious materials. The techno-dreams informing AI, for example, rehearse all the traditional repertoire of what was once considered angelic intelligence and corporeality. Craftsmanship, too, works with a notion of perfection just as any art form aspires to express a purity of communication in and through the medium it works with. Poetry employs rhythm, images, syntax, and the musical inherent in shaping any word to apprehend more than can be comprehended (to echo Shakespeare).

[9] The translation *On Music* is taken from (Augustine 2014). The Latin text is via Thesaurus Musicarum Latinarum project of Indiana University http://boethius.music.indiana.edu/tml/3rd-5th/.

the first provides the condition for the second. And in a further transformation, the composition of the movement in the *podus* becomes numerical: the movement from 1 to 2. Again, the association here between metrics and mathematics is found in Latin. Music "is the science of mensurating well (*scientia bene modulandi*)," Augustine writes[10]. The translation 'mensurating' is awkward, but *modulari* is the measurement of the change in rhythm, and in all things created (by God and Fabricated by humankind), Augustine writes, "measure must be observed[11]." This idea is then developed into music, for music "is the science of moving well. But that is because whatever moves and keeps harmoniously the measuring of times and intervals can already be said to move well[12]." That "keeps harmoniously" is "*numerose servatis*"—meaning "observing numbers" or "serving rhythm[13]." I will say more about the translation and use of 'harmony' later. For now, the point is: the anatomy of ambulation subscribes to a rhythm that is both mathematical and metrical: pure number is the basis of rhythm, for Augustine. Creation dances and all our movement moves within and participates in that *choresis*.

Over the next five books of *De musica*, the teacher takes the student from two-beat syllabic feet to highly complex metrical forms found in Latin poets from Vergil to Pindar to Horace, but with each level of complexity building upon the move from 1 to 2. This is the basis of all 'order' within creation and among created entities; the order of movement and temporality as such; the order that guarantees the meaningful. Much later in *De trinitate*, Augustine reflects, theologically, on this relation because 1 and 2 make 3[14]. This gets translated into the movement of the Father to the Son as second person of the Trinity, to the Holy Spirit that governs the unity of 1 and 2. Scholars will often refer to this as Augustine's number mysticism, but 'mysticism' is too loose and enigmatic a term. To call earthly life in its cosmological context 'creative' is to subscribe to its existence as meaningful and ordered, rather than a blind throw of the evolutionary dice—where 'evolution' embraces the origins and development of the observable universe. The 'destructive' belongs to what is evil and has no ontological substance. It is *inanis*. What Augustine is exploring is the nature of the ordering that opens the requirement to *make sense* that emerges from terrestrial movement, and all the rhythms of and in relations to such movement. He explores, that is, our total dependency upon the more primordial rhythm of Trinitarian life: a dependency in which the contingencies of creation rest within and upon that which is eternal and uncreated. And Augustine does this in *De musica* not by starting from any creedal assertion or divine revelation, but by starting from our listening to the world, and training the student, through getting him to clap or thump out the beats, to feel and participate in the rhythmic. To participate in the rhythmic is the basis of *making sense*, which, as I said, is the basis for the human activities of technological advancement, aesthetic production, and craftsmanship.

So much for an examination of "observing numbers" or "serving rhythm," but there is a word in that description of music that is even more fundamental (from a theological perspective) than "*numerose servatis*." For whatever moves does not just measure and subscribe to time, it engages "intervals" ("*atque intervallorum*")[15]. You have to shape and sound the word *intervallum* to get at something Augustine finds here. It's onomatopoeic. He is suspicious of vision as a sense because the orders of imagery and the operation of the imagination it invokes can be deceptive, theologically: the divine is not to be seen. We walk with that which is, at its most subtle level, unseen. The imagination

---

10 *De musica*, p. 172/2.
11 Ibid. p. 173/3.
12 Ibid. p. 175/3.
13 Whatever the relationship between rhythm, number, and meter, *numeros* as translating the Greek *rythmos* and *eurythmia* is central to Cicero's *Orator* as a necessary characteristic of prose. See (Hutchinson 2018) on 'Rhythmic Prose in Greek Imperial Literature'.
14 (Hill 1991). For the Latin text, see http://www.thelatinlibrary.com/august.html.
15 Augustine attention to "intervals of time [*temporalia intervalla*]" play an important theological role in *De trinitate*. He uses the term to distinguish the difference between human beings subject to contingency and God with whom "there are no intervals of time" (*op. cit.*, p. 430). Theologically this means, for him, that the whole of Trinity is involved in creation, incarnation, and redemption and there can be no thinking of 'first born' with respect to the Son and the Father outside of the human appeal to metaphor.

can mislead and become *phantasia*[16]. The auditory and the tactile he trusts more; they root both his physiology and psychology, and in the mouth-shaping that words require (he still belonged to a deeply oral culture) and by the breathings that give expression to those words the internal meets the external. *Intervallum*, as a word that is heard, begins with a short, stressed vowel and descends from there to an open, sonorous 'u' that's muted with the 'm'. It gives itself sonically and rhythmically to silence. And it is the silent, unseen and unheard, nature of the interval that Augustine reflects upon[17].

For Augustine, the Arabic 0 was not available as a mathematical order, so the dactylic and the iambic both register the movement from 1 to 2, and yet constitute a single foot. The movement from 1 to 2 both elides and requires an interval; but an interval traversed. The interval is a silence that points in two antithetical ways to Augustine: both to the 'nothing' out of which creation emerges and the continual present in which God alone dwells. The interval is a place where paradox is felt as the tension between 'emptiness' and 'plentitude'; an absence registered in the created order of things and the eternal presence of God. It is a space of distention that Augustine will develop later (in the *Confessions*, for example) into an account of time. Movement is inseparable from his thinking about time; our temporal condition as it is always open to contingent differences.

Why is this interval so important theologically? Because it opens the rhythms of creation in which living bodies are continually seeking some equilibrium between the internal and the external, biologically and mentally, to a divine rhythm as felt, not understood; groped at not grasped. And, in my analysis, this is where we encounter revelation—though not in any unmediated, unnuanced understanding of that term. For, throughout the Hebrew and the Christian Bible, one rhythm predominates to describe relations between the divine and human: the up/down, the down/up (similar in structure to the iambic and dactylic meters in prosody). It is most emphatic in Christological reflections: the incarnation/resurrection; the assumption/Pentecost. St. Paul frequently makes reference to this rhythm: notably in what is called the *Carmen Christi* of *Philippians* 2 and *Ephesians* 4. Here we have the twinning of *kenosis*/*pleroma* (emptying/filling), *anabasis*/*katabasis* (ascent/descent). Measured temporally and historically, these are two moments of a single wave function. Measured eternally, the two moments are one. That is, in the triune nature of God there is no up or down, but rather a perichoresis of persons in an endless reciprocal exchange of love. This perichoresis is what Dante figures as interlocked rings in the final canto of his *Commedia*. This divine rhythm constitutes what Augustine will call the *ordo amoris*, the order or rule of love that governs all things "in heaven and upon the earth." It is a hidden and transcendent *ordo*, though it is accommodated in some fitting manner to the created order because creation is in some sense *in God*. In God and through God all things came to be.

The 'interval' registers the tension of this eternal rhythm in time: hence, only paradoxes can define it. The 'interval' is what the human (the mammal?) brain cannot compute because the brain, in its pursuit of coherence, cannot consciously apprehend gaps[18]. It evolved as an organ that *makes* sense by ignoring and forgetting through the operation of attending to what is salient[19]. In the ongoing search for an equilibrium between the internal organism and its external environment, sense is made meaningful, and a coherent world-picture created, by conditioned pattern recognition, learnt responses, and the predictions of what to expect that these functions afford. This equilibrium between internal and external rhythms would all come under "*numerose servatis*," for Augustine. The way of religious faith is a walking

---

[16] In *De trinitate*, Augustine is much more positive about the creative powers of the imagination.

[17] In music, of course, the 'interval' can be given a certain signature. The composer Arvo Pärt extends the intervals until the point when, sometimes (in *Tabula Rasa*, for example), we are not sure the music will ever emerge again from the interval.

[18] Ellis and Solms, *op. cit.*, pp. 29–30: "the brain is essentially an organ of *prediction* ... what appears to be sensory perceptions are actually the brain's constructions of a representation of reality on the basis of what it expects to be there ... The mind creates an ongoing picture of the world on the basis of its expectations."

[19] The essential nature of human forgetting, that Augustine reflected upon in *Confessions*, is erased in notions of AI and all those fantasies of downloading the human mind onto a computer. Interestingly, in Jonathan Nolan's *Westworld*, the 'hosts' begin their evolution and adaptation through reverie and remembering.

with the invisible—the not seen or heard or touched or smelt or tasted. The way of life, the modes of behavior, formed in engaging with what is given in the 'interval' points beyond evolution. It is not antithetical to it; we fittingly evolved as creatures through it. But while love might be reduced to a reproductive strategy for survival of the species, neither faith nor hope (both existential investments in the unseen and both with affective correlations) seems to me simply responses to evolutionary demands. Of course, this is not to say that faith and hope are not instinctive correlatives of our seeking and wanting, and subsequently developed into more sophisticated behaviors as we acquire the "social brain[20]." But both faith and hope are modified, and impact behavior differently, when there is no visible direct object to which they are related or can be related. This needs considerably more development because, at the instinctive level, there are no specific objects sought (according to Panksepp).

We hopefully can now appreciate why Augustine does not use the term *harmonia* despite English-speaking translators[21]. The Pythagoreans, and later the Stoics, developed 'harmony' cosmologically. It expressed the primordial unity of part to whole. It could not treat dissonance as anything other than disturbance and, therefore, wrong; something to be overcome. But *intervallum* emphasizes that creation began and unfolded through separations, and the premiere separation establishes a rhythmic order beyond the created order[22]; a separation in which the Uncreated Creator is announced in the invisibility of Triune presence. Between the divine and the created, there can, then, only be *con-sonantia* (sounding together) or *con-gruentia* (meeting with—from *con* [with] and *ruere* [to fall]). That is, where the measures and movements of creation and all forms of human creativity engage with, and participate in, its Creator. Here, by faith (for this is a matter of entrusting to that which is not there as such), *ratio* (as reason) finds its higher and consummating proportionality in Christ as Logos—the divine *ratio* written into the created orders.

4. Conclusions

The effect of these operations, with respect to Augustine, meaning, and aesthetic activity, is that while we are continually *making* sense, the meaning of this sense is deferred. As he writes in *De civitati dei*, human beings have to make judgments and, simultaneously, have to declare an ignorance until the Day of Judgment. Meaning is no grand design in which we are all housed. So what remains is the meaningful, the pursuit of meaning as it dynamically unfolds through time and our aesthetic expressivity. The meaningful and aesthetic are continually emerging. But to the extent that human beings are being formed and informed with respect to their relationship with God, and what I sometimes call (for shorthand) the 'kenotic rhythm'—whereby all human judgments bear an epistemological humility—then judgments (even the aesthetic judgements made in human creativity) are, by intention, faithful. There is a consonance.

Funding: This research received no external funding.

Conflicts of Interest: The author declares no conflict of interest.

References

Augustine, Saint. 2014. *The Immortality of the Soul: The Magnitude of the Soul—On Music—The Advantage of Believing, on Faith in Things Unseen*. Washington, DC: Catholic University of America Press.

---

[20] The social brain hypothesis is central to the Oxford anthropologist Robin Dunbar. See (Dunbar 2009).

[21] It is true he uses what might be understood as a synonym, *Concordia*, but, as with *congruentia* and *consonantia*, it is the suffix that is important here—the relation 'with'. *Harmonia* dissolves the relational as a part within the whole, whereas the suffix '*con*' establishes difference, distinction and relation.

[22] The first rhythm of the created order established with the separation of darkness and light, night and day (Gen.1.4). "Everything that God creates, including human existence, is determined by this polarity ... The separation of light and darkness sets in motion this rhythmic polarity which will always belong to creation. Time take precedence over space in P's presentation of creation; creation does not begin with the division of space, but with the division of night and day as the basis of time" (Westermann 1994). Subsequently, with the creation over six days, God's Word writes time into creation; time is intrinsic to the gift of life and therefore good.

Barrow, John D., and Frank J. Tipler. 1986. *The Anthropic Cosmological Principle*. Oxford: Oxford University Press.

Berridge, Kent C. 1996. Food reward: Brain substrates of wanting and liking. *Neuroscience and Behavioral Reviews* 20: 1–25. [CrossRef]

Calasso, Roberto. 2001. *Literature and the Gods*. New York: Vintage, pp. 160–61.

Chatterjee, Anjan. 2014. *The Aesthetic Brain: How We Evolved to Desire Beauty and Enjoy Art*. Oxford: Oxford University Press.

Damasio, Antonio. 2000. *The Feeling of What Happens: Body, Emotion and the Making of Consciousness*. London: Vintage.

De Chardin, Teilhard. 1964. *Le Milieu Divin: An Essay on the Interior Life*. London: Fontana Book.

Deacon, Terrence W. 2012. *Incomplete Nature: How Mind Emerged from Matter*. New York: W.W. Norton & Company, p. 137.

Dunbar, Robin Ian MacDonald. 2009. The Social Brain Hypothesis and Its Implications for Social Evolution. *Annals of Human Biology* 36: 562–72. [CrossRef] [PubMed]

Eikelboom, Alexandria. 2018. *A Theological Category*. Oxford: Oxford University Press.

Ellis, George, and Mark Solms. 2017. *Beyond Evolutionary Psychology: How and Why Neuropsychological Modules Arise*. Oxford: Oxford University Press, pp. 83–103.

Fishbane, Michael. 2008. *Sacred Attunement: A Jewish Theology*. Chicago: Chicago University Press.

Frijda, Nico H. 2008. The Psychologists' Point of View. In *Handbook of Emotions*, 3rd ed. Edited by Michael Lewis, Jeanette M. Haviland-Jones and Lisa Feldman Barrett. New York: Guildford Press, pp. 68–87.

Gittings, Robert, ed. 1970. *Letters of John Keats*. Oxford: Oxford University Press, p. 43.

Hefner, Philip. 1993. *The Human Factor: Evolution, Culture, Religion*. Minneapolis: Fortress Press.

Hill, Edmund, trans. 1991, *The Trinity*. Book IV. 4–10. New York: New City Press, pp. 158–60.

Hutchinson, Gregory O. 2018. *Plutarch's Rhythmic Prose*. Oxford: Oxford University Press, pp. 1–27.

Kierkegaard, Søren. 1941. *Concluding Unscientific Postscript*. Translated by David F. Swenson and Walter Lowrie. Princeton: Princeton University Press, p. 178.

Panikkar, Raimon. 2010. *The Rhythm of Being: The Gifford Lectures*. New York: Orbis Books.

Panksepp, Jan. 1998. *Affective Neuroscience: The Foundations of Human and Animal Emotions*. Oxford: Oxford University Press.

Phelps, Elizabeth A. 2006. Emotion and Cognition: Insights from Studies of the Human Amygdala. *Annual Review of Psychology* 527: 27–53. [CrossRef] [PubMed]

Przywara, Erich. 2014. *Analogia Entis: Metaphysics: Original Structure and Universal Rhythm*. Translated by John Betz and David Bentley Hart. Grand Rapids: William B. Eerdmans.

Roberts, Jason. 2015. Fill and Subdue? Imaging God in New Social and Ecological Contexts. *Zygon* 50: 57. [CrossRef]

Sheets-Johnstone, Maxine. 2011. *The Primacy of Movement*, 2nd ed. Philadelphia: John Benjamins Publishing Company.

Tolkien, John Ronald Reuel. 2008. On Fairy Stories. In *Tolkien on Fairy Stories*. Edited by Verlyn Flieger and Douglas A. Anderson. London: HarperCollins, pp. 27–84.

Westermann, Claus. 1994. *Genesis 1-11*. Translated by John J. Scullion. Minneapolis: Fortress Press, p. 114.

Article

"He Who Sees Does Not Desire to Imagine": The Shifting Role of Art and Aesthetic Observation in Medieval Franciscan Theological Discourse in the Fourteenth Century

Oleg Bychkov

Theology Department, Saint Bonaventure University, St Bonaventure, NY 14778, USA; obychkov@sbu.edu

Received: 13 February 2019; Accepted: 13 March 2019; Published: 18 March 2019

Abstract: In the thirteenth century, following Neoplatonic and Patristic trends, art and aesthetic experience were still treated as symbolic, as "vestiges" or "echoes" of the divine that lead us to it. However, in the early fourteenth century, attitudes to concrete sensory/aesthetic experience begin to shift and theologians adopted the model of concrete phenomenal observation of sensory experience. Concrete sensory-aesthetic experience is endowed with a much higher value: seeing something is not the same as imagining it, recalling it, or thinking about it. This new approach results in some heterodox views about our phenomenal experience and debates about the exact status of "intentional" (phenomenal) appearance. These debates lead to profound observations about the nature of aesthetic-sensory experience of art objects and a re-evaluation of the status of the artistic image, which is now seen as much more than the platonic "copy of a copy". In other words, starting with the fourteenth century, theologians start to pay attention to concrete aesthetic (sensory) experience and use their observations to make conclusions about various cognitive and perceptual issues that could be relevant to a discussion of the divine. That is, quite separately from theoretical theological observations, art and aesthetic experience now provide independent approaches to the divine or spiritual via the experience of aesthetic wonder as a starting point. It is now our concrete experience of sensory and aesthetic objects that starts the train of thought, at times leading to some unorthodox conclusions that contradict the doctrine (such as the skeptical point of view). The intellectual shift in treating sensory and artistic objects in the fourteenth century invites some parallels with the current discussions of the experience of aesthetic wonder in "post-secular" thought.

Keywords: concepts: image; art; aesthetic; post-secular; wonder; Franciscan theology; intentionality; sensory experience

A brief look at the cultural history of humanity, from Australian aboriginals, who, through their unbroken tribal tradition, provide a snapshot of humanity as it was 50,000 years ago[1], to nineteenth century Europe, suggests that religion, in its broadest sense as human belief in a reality beyond this one, and the arts, in their broadest sense as human aesthetic expression, have been forever linked. While the arts and aesthetic expression have maintained their important position in human culture, in recent centuries, religion has been losing ground to a secular mentality, and the arts have been partly divorced from religion. Since the time of European Romanticism and its echoes in North America in the early nineteenth century, the arts and aesthetic experience have been increasingly presented as a new religion or a substitute for religion. In the past few decades, the idea of a post-secular mentality

---

[1] As an example, see the use of art by Australian Aboriginals in the National Geographic documentary *Australia's Aborigines* (NGHT, Inc., 2009).

was floated in Anglo-American intellectual circles[2]. Dissatisfied with the disenchantment of secular life, with its reductionist scientific picture of the world—with no God, no self[3], and sometimes not even consciousness in the picture, and with the determinist view that leaves no space for free will or any purpose to our existence—the post-secular person craves a re-enchantment of the world[4]. The post-secular sentiment rides the boundary between the secular and the religious, often capitalizing on phenomena that are part of everybody's secular experience and yet are somehow suggestive of something going beyond it, and thus quasi-religious. One of such phenomena is wonder or amazement in the face of the world—either its sheer existence or its intricate patterns[5]. The arts and aesthetic experience, once again, play a major role in eliciting the emotion of wonder, as the arts have traditionally made us aware of both the sheer fact of the existence of objects, and of beautiful patterns that suggest a regular organization of the universe based on eternal and universal laws, which are revealed to us by means of our reaction of wonder and aesthetic pleasure. In view of the developing post-secular mentality, and the quasi-religious role of the arts in it, the question is, if one looks at the history of human appreciation of the arts, when exactly the arts and aesthetic experience begin to be used autonomously or independently from theoretical theological observations to provide independent approaches to the divine or spiritual via the experience of aesthetic wonder as a starting point. The essay will focus on one specific period in medieval intellectual history, the early to mid-fourteenth century, when theological debates on the nature of sensory perception between several prominent Franciscan theologians, such as Peter Aureol (d. 1322), William Ockham (d. 1347), Walter Chatton (d. 1343), and Adam Wodeham (d. 1358), seem to shift the paradigm of how the arts are treated in a religious context and herald a new approach to secular art and secular experiences of art under a theological angle.

1. Toward a New Theory of the Image

In European scholarship, both Western and Eastern, much has been attributed to the supposed "secularization" of religious art in Western Christianity after Carolingian theologians reject both its sacred status and the iconoclastic position in the *Libri Carolini* (790) and at the Frankfurt Council (794): the position that supposedly both protected the use of art in religion and at the same time liberated it from its sacred-symbolic role and its rigid traditional iconographic types employed by Eastern Christianity[6]. However, all evidence, both iconic and textual, suggests the contrary. First, medieval Western Christian art pretty much sticks to rigid iconographic types up to the mid or even late thirteenth century. One needs only a quick look at religious images from that era, e.g., at newly created images of St. Francis, such as the Bardi dossal, to notice that they look very much like Eastern icons.[7] What is more important is that the theology of the image until the mid and even late thirteenth century remains very traditional. Let us take as an example the Franciscan order, which develops a theology that is most sensitive to aesthetic issues. (The reasons for this are Francis's own sensitivity to the

---

2   e.g., see Levine 2011; Warner et al. 2010.

3   This is a rather common, if shocking, view held by many contemporary neuroscientists and neuropsychologists, a typical example being David Eagleman, see: Eagleman 2011, and Eagleman 2017, pp. 75–106.

4   See Taylor 2011.

5   See Costa 2011. On the concept of wonder further see: Attfield 2018; Willmott 2018; Vasalou 2015.

6   For the supposed impact of the Libri Carolini and the Frankfurt Council on Western religious art, see: Quenot 1996, pp. 72–83; Sendler 1999, pp. 28–30. An immense literature in languages other than English exists on the practice of following traditional iconographic types in the Eastern Orthodox tradition, which is often called canonicity or canon. The practice can be documented textually in great detail starting with the sixteenth century, but elements of it are reflected in texts as early as the seventh century, and the pictorial evidence is obvious throughout the history of Orthodoxy. In English, see: Quenot 1996, pp. 66–72; Sendler 1999, pp. 19–21; Evdokimov 1996, pp. 213–17.

7   There are many historical reasons for that, such as that many Eastern iconographers fled to Italy during iconclastic persecutions, and that Franciscans specifically during the period of the Crusades had icon workshops in the Holy Land and the Latin Empire of Constantinople, which were directly impacted by local iconographers. However, this does not explain the persistence of rigid iconographic types in the West, since Western Christians supposedly had a choice not to follow these practices or not to employ Eastern-style iconographers.

material world and the Augustinian and Dionysian sources of early Franciscan theology). Franciscan theology engages a number of aesthetic issues, such as the beauty of the universe and of Christ as early as in the so-called *Sum of Theology of Alexander of Hales*.[8] Bonaventure is probably the most aesthetic of early Franciscan theologians.[9] However, Bonaventure's schema in the mid to late thirteenth century still reflects the traditional view of art formulated in Christian Patristic theology. His position on the role of images in churches is reminiscent of John Damascene's standard opinion against iconoclasts: they serve as "visual scriptures" for the illiterate, excite affection, and assist memory; the honor paid to the picture goes back to the prototype. His theology elaborates somewhat on this standard view, but still goes no further than professing the symbolic role of artistic images: like other material things, they are echoes and vestiges of the divine. From Augustine he borrows the idea of the transcending movement of the mind, which begins with perceiving patterns in physical reality by using one's aesthetic sense and ends with a realization of their eternal God-like nature. From contemporary perspectivists he borrows the theory of the sensory form (*species*) of a material thing in the mind and applies it to the second person of the Trinity. Just as the sensory *species*, which travels through various levels of reality, up to our intellect, and points back to its source, Christ as form-beauty (*species*), as the perfect likeness of the Father, points back to the Father.[10]

It seems that in order to see any real change in attitudes toward art and sensory-aesthetic experience in Western Christianity one needs to fast-forward to the fourteenth century. Once again, what follows is based on the Franciscan theological tradition. Following Peter John Olivi and John Duns Scotus's emphases on the role of concrete sensory experience in constructing cognitive and epistemological sections of theology[11], Franciscan theologians of the fourteenth century abandon the religious-symbolic view of art and natural beauty and begin to pay attention to specific sensory experiences—which are equally available to secularly-minded individuals—and the way they allow one to fine-tune one's cognitive theory. One sees a rising number of references to sensory experience, a frequent use of aesthetic comparisons that involve concrete aesthetic experiences, including those of art objects (and not just symbolic interpretations of art or abstract examples), and a development of fine theological points based on these concrete experiences, and not stemming from preconceived theological notions about art and aesthetics. It seems that to Franciscan theologians from the fourteenth century, sensory and aesthetic experiences were the source of a genuine intellectual wonder that triggered further insights into the nature of our perception of what we call "reality": an important preliminary step in any medieval commentary on the *Sentences* prior to embarking on an exploration of the divine.

2. The Importance of Sensory Experience

As part of the preliminary discussion of the range and possibilities of human cognition, including the possibility of cognition of the divine, theologians in the fourteenth century faced a major epistemological hurdle—and it is precisely sensory and aesthetic experience that was called upon in Franciscan theology to clear it. The problem they faced was that the reliability of sensory perception and phenomenal experience was threatened by the 63rd proposition of the condemnations of 1277, which rejected the thesis that "God cannot produce the effect of a secondary cause without the secondary cause itself"[12]. The position implied that all of our sensory and phenomenal experiences at least in principle could exist without any real things standing behind them, because God can simulate them for our mind. Several major Franciscan theologians, such as Peter Aureol, William

---

[8]   See Bychkov 2010, pp. 271, 301–2.
[9]   See Bychkov 2013; Bychkov 2010, pp. 268–321.
[10] In addition to Bychkov (2013) see *Sent*. III, dist. 9, art. 1, qu. 2 (III, 202-5). Bonaventure's works are cited according to the "great" Quaracchi edition.
[11] See Olivi's *Sent*. II, q. 57, in Olivi 1924. On Scotus, see Bychkov 2014.
[12] See Denifle and Châtelain 1889, p. 547.

Ockham, Walter Chatton, and Adam Wodeham, rely on sensory and aesthetic experience to argue about this issue. Several major positions develop on the issue of reliability of sensory experience between these four theologians. Aureol insists that some special mode of being is at play, which he calls variously "intentional", "apparent", "conspicuous" and so on, to account for the phenomenal appearances of things to our minds that seemingly can exist without any "real" things standing behind them—not only under God's hypothetical influence but even naturally. Common proofs brought forth in support of this position are cases when we have phenomenal experiences of things that are not actually there, as when we experience sensory illusions, afterimages, and hallucinations. For example, according to Wodeham, who discusses this opinion (even though it is not his own), it could happen that "some [visual] elements of a currently present thing might be visible that mimic the shape of a rabbit or a castle when other elements are out of sight" and we actually take it for a rabbit or a castle[13]. Just about everybody else except Aureol denies the existence of this special mode of being, but their positions on the status of phenomenal appearance vary[14]. While Ockham is a typical direct realist who simply postulates that unless there is some impediment, we perceive real things as they are in reality, and our sensory perception is absolutely trustworthy, most theologians, such as Chatton and Wodeham, assume a moderate stance: there is no intermediate being between our mind and real things, but our phenomenal perception of them can be affected in various ways by the conditions of perception and its interpretation by our mental faculties, which accounts for illusions and afterimages. Thus, our sensory perception can be trusted only for the most part, although this is sufficient for practical purposes.

In order to prove their points in the midst of this heated debate, all sides rely heavily on sensory experience. Thus Peter Aureol, defending his claim that even things that are not physically present can appear phenomenally to our mind, speaks of the "way of experience, to which one must adhere more than to any whatsoever logical arguments, because science begins with experience," and the "indication of truth in speech is its correspondence with things that are perceived by the senses"[15]. Although Ockham is radically opposed to Aureol's idea of apparent being, he also values actual sensory experience and its tight connection to our intellectual processes, except, according to him, it proves the opposite, that the process of sensory perception is direct and unmediated by any apparent being[16].

Chatton and Wodeham have, perhaps, the most extensive comments on the importance of sensory experience. Chatton's direct realist position, against that of Aureol, is that our phenomenal experience of objects of sensory perception is not some special kind of being, but the act of sensory perception itself, e.g., vision[17]. Chatton, as most of his contemporaries, is concerned with the certitude of the information delivered by the senses, because "we have maximal certitude about objects of sensory perception by virtue of the fact that we *experience* our sensory perceptions, through which objects of sensation appear to us as present"[18]. In his opinion, Aureol's model of apparent being inserts some sort of an intermediary between the object and the faculty of sensory perception and introduces skeptical doubt. In his defense of the role of sensory perception, Chatton goes further than his Franciscan predecessors and even denies the need for intellective intuitive cognition: a type of intellectual cognition that makes us aware of the immediate presence of objects of sense perception or mental activities. Most Franciscan theologians prior to Chatton, such as Scotus or Ockham, include this sort of cognition in their cognitive

---

13   *Lectura secunda* 1, prol., qu. 3, par. 8, in Wodeham 1990, p. 82.

14   The literature on the debate about "intentional being" is enormous, and there is no space in this essay to discuss the issue or even to cite all the literature. A concise account of the issue itself and of the complex palette of positions that develop around it in Franciscan thought in the fourteenth century is given in Bychkov 2018.

15   Aureol, *Scriptum* 1, Prooemium, Sectio Secunda, C., Resp., art. 3, n. 81, in Aureoli 1956, p. 198.

16   Cf. Ockham, *Ord.* 1, prol., q. 1, a. 1, in Ockham 1967, p. 38.10–11.

17   See Chatton, *Rep.* et *Lect.* 1, prol., q. 2, a. 2: "it creates less of a difficulty to concede that the 'objective being' of an extramental thing is the very act of vision," in Chatton 1989, p. 88.65–70; "the very cognition [of an extramental thing] can be called a 'being' of this object. This denomination does not concern anything internal [to the thing]. When it is used, what it means is that a thing is cognized; all it means is that this cognition is present in the soul" (Chatton 1989, p. 89.83–6).

18   Chatton, *Rep.* et *Lect.* 1, prol., q. 2, a. 2 (Chatton 1989, p. 89.91–5); my emphasis.

theory[19]. According to Chatton however, sensory intuitive cognition is all we need to verify the existence of an extramental object; this position, of course, radically increases the importance of sensory perception[20]. And yet, assuming a more moderate position compared to that of Ockham, Chatton does admit the fact of residual sensations, such as afterimages after having seen a bright object, even though he attempts to explain them away without using Aureol's model of apparent being[21].

While Chatton's concession implies (whether he likes the consequence or not) that sensory intuitive cognition provides no basis for certainty, Wodeham opposes even Chatton's concession. He contends that in the realm of nature, sensory intuitive cognition certifies the existence of extramental objects. His only concession, following the condemnation of 1277, is that God can simulate any sensory experience without extramental thing[22]. Reason and experience correct misleading appearances of "non-existent" things mentioned in Aureol's examples, and the senses ordinarily can be trusted, except under very unusual circumstances, such as divine interference. Like Chatton, Wodeham opposes Scotus and Ockham and denies the necessity of intellective intuitive cognition (*notitia incomplexa intuitiva*) that is different from sensation, claiming that sensory cognition is sufficient to assent to an object of sensory perception (*res sensibilis*)[23]. Wodeham's attempt to eliminate intellective intuitive cognition, of course, is aimed at eliminating uncertainty in sensory perception. The problem of how "physical" sensory material gets into a purely "spiritual" intellect remains unresolved in Aristotle and Aquinas[24]. However, if one argues for the unity of sensory and intellectual capacities, presenting them more like shades of the same rather than sharply divided, sensory cognition can account for the certainty of perception, as there is no need to "spiritualize" it in order to transfer it to the intellect. If there is only one perceptive power, there is no need to prove the reality of the extramental world to the intellect, and skepticism is eliminated. In fact, of course, neither side of the debate about the status of phenomenal appearances (Aureol vs. Ockham/Chatton/Wodeham) ultimately eliminates skeptical doubt. However, while attempting to do so, curiously, both sides elevate the importance of sensory experience to a much higher level.

---

19 Cf. Scotus, *Ord.* IV, d. 45, qq. 2–3, and Ockham, *Ord.* 1, prol., q. 1.
20 Chatton, *Rep. et Lect.* 1, prol., q. 2, a. 4 (Chatton 1989, p. 112.204–11): "it seems that in this life the soul naturally does not have any intuitive intellection [of sensibles], because exterior sensations are sufficient to it to cause any whatsoever assent to things signified by contingent propositions. Indeed, when the soul forms the compound proposition 'whiteness exists', while at the same time experiencing a sensory vision of whiteness, everything else having been circumscribed, the result is an assent to the thing that is signified by the contingent compound proposition 'whiteness exists'. Therefore, one ought not posit there any other [type of] intuitive cognition in respect to this [object] except for sensory vision."
21 Chatton, *Rep. et Lect.* 1, prol., q. 2, a. 2 (Chatton 1989, p. 91.150–58; cf. Chatton 1989, p. 95.255–66): "Indeed, on some occasions the vision that has been previously caused has a tendency to remain for some time after the object of vision has gone away. This is because the intense [visual] species, which immediately causes vision, remains for some time after the object of vision has gone away, on account of the intensity of this [visual] species. However, no vision ever has a tendency to be naturally caused or preserved for a long time without the presence of the object of vision... for neither is the [visual] species itself naturally caused nor remains for a long time without the thing of which it is the species....". Otherwise, Chatton cautions, we would not have any certitude about sensory objects caused by natural causes. These arguments, of course, do not make a good case against Aureol, because one still needs to account for where that residual image is, and Chatton fails to account at all for hallucinations. In fact, Chatton himself admits that even short residual sensations put a dent into his position by conceding that at the time when that residual vision remains, while the object has disappeared, "there is no certitude" (Chatton 1989, p. 92.175ff).
22 Wodeham, *Lectura secunda* 1, prol., qu. 2, par. 4–5 (Wodeham 1990, pp. 40–41).
23 Wodeham, *Lectura secunda* 1, prol., qu. 1, par. 2 (Wodeham 1990, pp. 9–10): intellective intuitive cognition would be required in order in ensure an "evident judgment about the existence of a sensory thing" and its contingent conditions. However, as things stand, it is not required, "because when something white is demonstrably visible, we accept an evident and certain assent of the intellect, by which it judges that this [sensory thing] exists." This judgment does not need any other simple intuitive knowledge apart from this "sensory vision," unless this vision is obscure or imperfect. This statement is repeated almost verbatim in Wodeham, *Lectura secunda* 1, prol., qu. 1, par. 4 (Wodeham 1990, p. 13), and is paraphrased in par. 11 (Wodeham 1990, p. 25). In fact, our sensory experience is so cognitive in nature that we routinely apply the language of intellection to it: "All our sensations are immediately received in the intellect and are acts of the intellect, although properly speaking no sensation is intellection.... Therefore all statements such as the following are true, even though only accidentally: 'the intellect knows something white by sensory vision' or '[the intellect knows] a sound by means of hearing'" (par. 5 [Wodeham 1990, p. 15]).
24 See Bychkov 2015.

Fascination with sensory experience in the fourteenth century, in fact, runs so high that Franciscan theologians often place it not only above the faculty of the imagination but even above the faculty of reason[25]. Thus Aureol, despite the main thrust of his theory of apparent being that presents all phenomenal experience, even under natural conditions, as mental simulation (to use a modern term) and thus seems to put the certainty of sensory perception into question, still values sensory or aesthetic experience (which he calls "intuitive knowledge") higher than the imagination or ideation, because it provides a more direct and vivid contact with the object of perception. Aureol, unlike Chatton or Wodeham, tries to defend the existence of intuitive intellective cognition in the mind. His line of argument proceeds as follows: if he can prove that intuitive cognition generally is superior to other forms of cognition, then the intellective faculty must include it. Aureol proves this by drawing an analogy between the operation of the intellective and sensory faculties. In the sensory faculty, the role of intuitive cognition falls to direct sensory perception, while the role of abstractive cognition to the imagination. Aureol's comparison between sensory perception and imagination turns into a kind of *apologia* of sensory perception: an intuitive or sensory knowledge of an object, such as a rose, is more desirable, delightful, clear, and certain than imagining the same object:

> For it is clear that intuitive [sensory] knowledge is more noble than the knowledge gained through the imagination [i.e., abstractive], on many accounts. First, because it is desirable. For a person who imagines something desires to see it; however, he who sees [something] does not desire to imagine [it]. Second, because it is more delightful. For it is more delightful to see a rose or a thing one loves than to imagine it. Third, because it is more clear. For the person who imagines a certain thing still experiences himself to remain somehow in the dark as regards this thing; however, he who sees [something, experiences] the clarity of knowledge in every respect. Fourth, because it is more certain. For vision is experiential knowledge, and imagination is not. And therefore [Aristotle] in Bk. 2 of *On the Soul* attributes truth to the senses and deception and proneness to error to the imagination. Fifth, it follows from the above that it is more perfect and ultimate, for it unites [the one who perceives] with the object [of perception] most perfectly and ultimately.[26]

Chatton seconds this evaluation: seeing or experiencing a thing in a sensory way is very different from just knowing or thinking about it. Chatton in this case argues against Ockham: while Ockham claims that science is about compound propositions about things (*complexum*), Chatton and Wodeham argue that science is about things themselves (in the case of Wodeham, more precisely, about both things themselves and propositions about them, which he calls "significative compounds"). Wodeham agrees with Chatton, and to prove the point he borrows his distinction between conclusions by demonstration and from experience. The two propositions (by demonstration and from experience) are not similar, even though they signify one and the same thing, but are "of a different nature":

> although he who actually sees a [real] thing would not necessarily form an abstractive concept [of it]... nevertheless, if he were to form it... that concept would be of a different nature compared to a concept that one forms when one does not see [this] thing. Otherwise already in this life we would form propositions about God that are as evident as those that the blessed form in the next. Now a conclusion that is a result of a [logical] demonstration is put together out of concepts that are formed without having seen the thing that causes [this

---

[25]   The trend is apparent already in Scotus, whose thought triggers many subsequent discussions. For example, according to Scotus, the reason that the sacraments are accompanied by sensory signs is that "we seek and desire more avidly that, which is known to us more clearly, for all our acquisition of knowledge in this earthly life originates with sensation; therefore, in order that we may seek and desire grace more intensely and fervently, it must be presented to us under a sensory sign" (*Reportatio* IV-A, dist. 26–28, Resp., Civitas Vaticana, bibl. apost., cod. vat. lat. 883, f. 286ra).

[26]   Aureol, *Scriptum* 1, Prooemium, Sectio Secunda, C., Resp., art. 4, n. 117 (Aureoli 1956, p. 208).

proposition]. However, a proposition that one forms after having experienced the thing is put together out of such concepts as the thing causes by means of vision.[27]

3. Intentional Objects and Images

Heated debates about apparent or intentional being between Aureol and his opponents simply bring into relief one more time that mysterious identity between real things and their phenomenal stand-ins that we perceive every day. Even Aureol's opponents acknowledge the capacity of phenomenal appearances in mental experience to create a vivid feeling that what we perceive are things "out there" in their "outerness". To use philosophical terminology, they create an "ontological commitment". In Aureol's words, "intellection seems to terminate at the [real] thing, and our gaze to observe the thing itself, and to glance over it as over an object that is [currently] in our presence", e.g., when we say "I understand, look at, or observe a rose"[28].

However, the most interesting observation for aesthetics that comes out of these debates against Aureol's model of intentionality is that it is not only phenomenal appearances of perceived things that can create this feeling of outerness and identity between phenomenal appearances and things that are perceived as extramental, but also phenomenal appearances of perceived images of things, such as their artistic representations. Thus Chatton, in the process of his debate against Aureol's apparent being, analyzes the example of "seeing" something in a dream.[29] According to Chatton, in such cases one does not see something non-existent (as allegedly Aureol claims), but something in the mental organ, which cannot be distinguished from, e.g., a vision of color. This explanation is not incongruous, because exactly the same thing happens in our experience of art: a picture is not a sensory vision of a real object, but it is perceived as such or substitutes for actual vision: e.g., when "someone sees a painted rose, this is not a vision of an [actual] rose, and yet he judges that he sees a rose" (Chatton 1989, p. 97.306-7). It is difficult not to see this statement as a sincere admission of the power of pictorial images that stems from real experience and is used to solve a difficult cognitive problem, as opposed to a mere case of using stock art examples from traditional symbolic theology. Chatton repeats the same example of perceiving a rose when he analyzes the difficult case of automatic neurocognitive reaction to certain shapes in our visual field, which even animals possess, e.g., when a sheep flees from something that is shaped like a wolf (even if it is not really a wolf, but, e.g., a sheep disguised as a wolf)[30]. As the case of a sheep fleeing from a sheep that looks like a wolf shows, such automatic reactions can also result in perceptual errors, which are brought forth to argue for or against the existence of the special mode of apparent being. This sort of perceptual reaction, Chatton explains, is not the same as intellectual judgment, but it is automatic, and therefore animals can have it, too. Chatton explains our automatic reaction as follows:

> A rose... commonly has properties of a certain kind, such as red color and five-leaflet leaves, and so forth. Therefore, when someone, after having experienced these properties on many occasions, sees from afar something that has these properties, he immediately judges that this object is a rose, even though it may not be a [real] rose but something painted to resemble a rose.[31]

Wodeham, engaging some of Chatton's points, such as his attempt to account for visual illusions, repeats Chatton's example of perceiving a painted rose that is taken for a real one. In visual illusions,

---

[27] Chatton, *Rep. et Lect.* 1, prol., qu. 4, a. 1 (Chatton 1989, p. 228.106–14), as quoted in Wodeham, *Lectura secunda* 1, dist. 1, qu. 2, par. 2, art. 1 (Wodeham 1990, pp. 211–12).

[28] Aureol, *Scriptum* 1, d. 27, p. 2, art. 2, in *The Peter Auriol Homepage* (text version of 20 July 2009, copyright R.L. Friedman, http://www.peterauriol.net/auriol-pdf/SCR-27-2.pdf), p. 12.427–32.

[29] Chatton, *Rep. et Lect.* 1, prol., q. 2, a. 2 (Chatton 1989, pp. 96–97).

[30] The example goes back to Avicenna's passage from a version of his commentary on Aristotle's *On the Soul*, Part 6 (available in Latin in the 1200–1300's), which was widely used in medieval Latin scholastic literature. See Avicenna 1982.

[31] Chatton, *Rep.* 1, dist. 3, q. 1, a. 2, ad 1, n. 41, in Chatton 2002, p. 219.

some "concurrent species" are involved that are similar to an external thing seen previously, "and therefore a thing is believed to be seen, which nevertheless is not [truly] seen. But this creates no more difficulty than the case when someone believes that he is seeing a real rose while in fact he is seeing merely a painted rose"[32]. The implication for aesthetics and art of this identity of intentional appearances of things with the things themselves is that it removes the difference—at least the phenomenal difference—between the real thing and its phenomenal appearance—in the mode of apparent being, Aureol would say—potentially giving images, and thereby also artistic images, a status that is much higher than that of classic Platonic "imitation." Phenomenal appearances of things in fact feel like things themselves. And since such phenomenal appearances could be generated by painted images as well as real things, the difference between phenomenal experiences generated by real objects and artistic representations is diminished: both processes go through the same mechanism of creating a phenomenal picture—or the mode of apparent being, if we side with Aureol. It is clear that this important revelation about the nature of pictorial images comes, once again, not from a symbolic-theological way of thinking about art but from direct observation of actual images with a subsequent phenomenological analysis of the experience. It is also important that the images in the examples are not of an explicitly religious kind: roses, castles, emperors, greyhounds, and rabbits mentioned in theological examples are obviously part of secular chivalric imagery.

Two examples illustrate the new approach to art in the fourteenth century, when theologians begin to use mundane (i.e., secular) observations about art, including secular art, to make theological points, in this case to argue for or against the existence of the special kind of "apparent being" in the human perceptual system. Both examples are of everyday art that one would encounter in their day-to-day life, not specifically of symbolic religious art.

4. The Example of Stained Glass

One of the persistent examples in Franciscan theology in the fourteenth century is light passing through stained glass windows: to be sure, an actual daily experience for the religious at that time. Franciscans have been involved with stained glass and commented on it at least since the times of Bonaventure[33]. Bonaventure himself mentions stained glass in the Narbonne Constitutions of the Franciscan Order produced in 1260 under his leadership and occasionally illustrates his theological points using the example of stained glass windows. However, he uses stained glass examples in exactly the same way as he uses iconic images: to make a point about the theological symbolism of the created world that points to the divine. Thus in the *Collations on the Six Days of Creation* (*Collationes in Hexaemeron* 12.14; V, 386b) Bonaventure uses stained glass symbolically to convince the reader of the existence of God's "exemplary reasons" (commonly known as divine ideas). There are several "aids for us to ascend to exemplary reasons". The first is "sensory creatures":

> The entire world is a shadow, path, vestige, and the book written on the outside. For every creature contains a refulgence of the divine exemplar, even though it is mixed with darkness [there]; therefore, it is as if some opaqueness were mixed with light. Also, it is a path that leads one to the exemplar. Just as, from your observation, a ray [of sunlight] that enters through a [stained glass] window is colored in various ways according to the various colors of the different shards of [stained] glass, in the same way the divine ray shines in different ways in the various properties of individual creatures.

Stained glass continues to fascinate Franciscan theologians in the fourttenth century. However, the way they use the example of stained glass changes dramatically. Instead of merely pointing out

---

[32] Wodeham, *Lectura secunda* 1, prol., qu. 3, par. 8 (Wodeham 1990, p. 81).
[33] Thus Angela of Foligno records the presence of stained glass in the Basilica of St. Francis in Assisi in mid-thirteenth century: "I saw a stained-glass window depicting St. Francis being closely held by Christ" (Lachance 1993, p. 141). On Franciscans and stained glass see: Thompson 2016.

some symbolism in a stock example, they seem to be mesmerized with their actual experience of colored light and draw on their actual observations—without any connection to existing theological positions—to make various points about human cognitive mechanisms. For example, Chatton and Wodeham's polemic against Aureol results in several sharp observations about the mechanism of sensory perception and phenomenal appearance as they attempt to explain away various perceptual examples that seem to suggest the existence of the special mode of apparent being. One such example relevant to aesthetics is the perception of a color patch on the wall or floor of a church after the sunlight has passed through a piece of stained glass in the church window. What exactly is the status of this observable patch of color? Is it the colored glass that we see? Is it the sun? Or is it just some redness? One of the examples in favor of the existence of apparent being has been that we experience afterimages after having seen a bright object, even after this object is no longer present. Rejecting Aureol's model of "apparent being", Wodeham sides with Chatton in affirming that afterimages are not as clear and not quite the same as when the object is actually in the line of sight.[34] He attributes these afterimages to the impact of the residual sensory form (*species*) in the mind, which does not create the same sort of clarity as the presence of an actual object of vision. Re-examining the example of light passing through a stained glass window used by Ockham and Chatton, Wodeham observes that "the fact that I see redness that is produced on the wall from the passing of the ray of the sun through red [stained] glass does not make me conclude that I see the glass but only that I see that redness". This is exactly what happens when we experience afterimages: we see residual sensory species of sensory objects, not objects themselves (Wodeham 1990, p. 76). What allows us to avoid perceptual error in this case is the fact that, in addition to detecting color and shape, our vision also includes situational awareness, in this case the perception that there is no direct line of sight to the object of vision, which saves us from the error of "seeing" the original object in the case of an afterimage. Our vision takes into consideration the position of the body vis-à-vis the object:

> Now what one sees there is the species, namely, the redness that is caused by the passing ray of light, and the redness of the glass does not appear to me on this account. For this reason one can make an argument that it also does not appear to me in another situation [i.e., when there is a direct line of sight to the primary object] that I see the principal thing merely because I see its species, but that something else [here] is added to the cause [of the apparition], let's say a powerful image of that principal thing in the imagination that concurs [with the species]. However, no such thing concurs [with the species] in this case [when there is no direct line of sight to the object of vision], and therefore it does not appear to me that I see the glass. Indeed, what prevents the error of [perceptual] judgment in this case is that, with only the species being present, the [physical] position [of the observer], which is out of alignment with the principal object of vision, blocks the direct line of sight, and therefore [also blocks] the [formation of the] image in the imagination [from that principal object of vision].[35]

The example of light passing through a stained glass window, of course, can be interpreted in the opposite way: seeing redness on the wall does alert us both to the existence of a stained glass window and to the fact that the sun is out. However, it is the fact itself that Franciscan theologians make fine conceptual points using an analysis of an actual aesthetic experience of an art object that is important here.

---

[34] Wodeham, *Lectura secunda* 1, prol., qu. 3, par. 7 (Wodeham 1990, p. 75).
[35] Wodeham, *Lectura secunda* 1, prol., qu. 3, par. 8 (Wodeham 1990, p. 78).

5. The Example of the Image of the Emperor

Fourteenth-century Franciscans are equally keen on using examples of painted images, of the type they must have observed in the form of frescoes on walls of buildings. It is important that the example discussed below is not of a religious, but of a secular image, perhaps seen in a palace. The example is used in the discussion about the status of pictorial representations, which is part of the discussion of "apparent" or "intentional" being among Franciscan theologians. Both Aureol and Wodeham bring up the artistic-aesthetic example of the depiction of the emperor on the wall, which appears as early as in the writings of Scotus's secretary William of Alnwick[36]. Each uses the example in defense of his own theory: Aureol in defense of apparent being and Wodeham against this model. Aureol must defend his theory against the opinion that phenomenal appearances give no more being to their objects than an image of the emperor on the wall gives to the emperor. He describes the opinion as follows: "a thing conceived [by the mind] only receives its *name* from the act of the intellect and does not acquire any intentional being, any more than the emperor acquires [any being] from his depiction if he is painted"[37]. Wodeham is one of the theologians who support this opposing opinion. His point is that "the emperor" in the picture is just a metaphorical denomination, because one only deals with the real emperor when one is in contact with the real object of perception, a real person in this case:

> an extramental thing, whether it exists or not, has no being whatsoever by virtue of being cognitively perceived—neither in the mind nor outside the mind, and neither in a qualified sense nor in a non-qualified sense—just as neither does the emperor have any being whatsoever by virtue of being painted... However, in both cases—when the emperor is referred to as painted or an object of cognition is referred to as cognized—something (the emperor or the object of cognition) receives its external name from something else (picture or cognitive act).[38]

For "the emperor to be depicted" amounts to nothing more than the "existence of a picture which was created for the purpose of reminding us of the emperor" (Wodeham 1990, pp. 89–90).

Although Aureol disagrees with the position that equates the status of phenomenal appearance with the status of depicted images of objects, in his debates against this objection he does not disagree with the assessment of painted images as inferior to mental representations. Indeed,

> [for a thing] to receive one's name from something does not amount to being present or manifest to the thing that gives this [original thing] its name, nor to be observed by it, nor to be in its line of sight, nor to occur to it, nor to be placed over and against it—just as it is clear that if the emperor is painted, [the emperor] is not present or manifest to the picture [or the wall], nor is observed by it, nor is in its line of sight, nor occurs to it, nor is placed over and against it. However, our experience teaches us that if a thing is cognitively perceived, it is manifest and present to the intellect that perceives it, and occurs to it, is observed by it, and is in its line of sight. Therefore, it not only receives its name [from the phenomenal apparition] but also some intentional being.[39]

---

[36] Cf. Perler 2001, p. 220.

[37] *Scriptum* 1, d. 23, a. 2, in Pinborg 1980, p. 135; my italics.

[38] *Lectura secunda* 1, prol., qu. 4, par. 3 (Wodeham 1990, pp. 89–90).

[39] Petrus Aureoli, *Scriptum* 1, d. 23, a. 2, in Pinborg 1980, p. 136. The same example is repeated in *Scriptum* 1, d. 27, p. 2, art. 2, in *The Peter Auriol Homepage*, p. 11.395-6, and in the answer to the 4th objection, *The Peter Auriol Homepage*, p. 16.572-75, 81–82: a thing that is understood does not receive merely its name in the process of intellection, "as the emperor from a painting [of him] or something represented [in a picture] from its representation: for the emperor himself is not present to the wall through a picture [of him], nor is he placed over and against it, nor does [the wall] judge about him [variant: about his existence], unlike things that are present to the intellect [in phenomenal apparitions]... and yet every one who uses his intellect experiences a thing present to his intellect, when he thinks about it; therefore this sort of being [i.e., intentional] does not amount to receiving a name". Also cf. *Scriptum* 1, d. 35, q. 1, a. 1, in *The Peter Auriol Homepage*, ll. 326–36: "Similarly, if the emperor painted on a wall appeared [phenomenally] to the wall through a picture [of him] painted on this wall, one could say that this wall would be cognitively aware of the painted emperor".

Now both Wodeham in opposing Aureol, and Aureol in defending against this specific point—namely that an image or depiction of something does not make that thing present to the medium where it is depicted, while when we intellectually or sensorily perceive something, the thing itself is present to our mind—miss the point of artistic representations, formerly attested to by Chatton and Wodeham himself, namely that they make things appear to *us*, not to the medium. Aureol, however, corrects the situation elsewhere, ascertaining the real purpose of images, when he uses the example of the depiction of the emperor to support his theory that there is some mental substrate underlying our phenomenal pictures, even though it is not perceived as such, but creates an impression of extramental things being present to us[40]. It is the same with pictorial representations:

> a real picture relates to [giving] depicted being [to something] in the same way as a real [phenomenal] apparition relates to giving apparent being [to something]. However, the emperor would never acquire depicted being except insofar as there is some real picture [of him]. Therefore, nor will [real] things appear to the intellect except insofar as there are some formal and real apparitions [of them] in the intellect (*The Peter Auriol Homepage*, ll. 370-3).

As such the purpose of pictorial representations is different: just as in the case of a special kind of mental substrate that makes a thing appear to us phenomenally, a picture makes a thing or a person appear to us as well. In the absence of pictures, we would merely have abstract thoughts about persons and things, not their "presential" (Aureol's term) perception.

No matter what the particular claims of Franciscan theologians are, their discussion reveals something fundamental about the status of the artistic image, as well as, generally, the status of the phenomenal. Wodeham's point is that "the emperor" in the picture is just a metaphorical denomination, because one only deals with the real emperor when one is in contact with the real person. However, Aureol would say that our experience of "real" things from the point of view of the mental mechanisms involved is not all that different from our experience of images: in either case all we see is an apparent being (*ens visum* or *manifestum*). Artistic images thus cannot be regarded by default as a "lower" form of delivering phenomenal experience. In fact, even Chatton and Wodeham admit that a picture of an object or a person can create an impression of a real presence of an object or a person through the image, as in the example of a painted rose above. In other words, contact through a picture does not have to be less real than contact through a sense perception of a "real object," because both processes ultimately result in phenomenal appearances (or "apparent being," according to Aureol).

6. Secularization of Art?

It is becoming abundantly clear, then, that while Bonaventure's understanding of the role of artistic images, artifacts, and aesthetic experience in the thirteenth century remains squarely within the realm of symbolic theology or the Patristic theology of the icon, new cognitive models in the Franciscan psychology and philosophy of perception in the fourteenth century begin to rely on the actual experience of artifacts and images for new insights. Thus in the fourteenth century, art in theology is no longer used as sacred or symbolic, but in a "secular" fashion: as arousing one's intellectual wonder and curiosity. Instead of sacred symbols, artistic images and artifacts turn into contemplative tools. One can only wonder whether this attitude was inspired by the new style in art, such as that of Giotto's increased realism, or shepherded this style, to turn art into a meditative tool to wonder at and draw insights, instead of using it symbolically to direct our mental gaze at the prototype, while ignoring all the intricacies of the sensory perception of the actual art object in front of us. This wonder at the sight of an artistic image (which mysteriously makes objects appear before

---

[40]   *Scriptum* 1, d. 9, q. 1. a. 1, in *The Peter Auriol Homepage*, ll. 364-9: "A thing cannot possess an apparent being of this kind except by virtue of some real absolute [substrate] that exists in the intellect."

our mental gaze and makes us think about cognitive mechanisms) or at the play of colored light in a cathedral (which makes us wonder about the mysteries of sensory perception), to be sure, is used in theological discourse about the divine. But the inspiration for this discourse is no longer merely scriptures and sacred symbols, but also our sensory and cognitive experiences of this reality, which is produced by the power of both God and art.

Funding: This research received no external funding.

Conflicts of Interest: The author declares no conflict of interest.

References

Attfield, Robin. 2018. *Wonder, Value, and God*. London and New York: Routledge.

Aureoli, Peter. 1956. *Scriptum Super Primum Sententiarum*. Edited by Eligius M. Buytaert. St. Bonaventure: The Franciscan Institute, vol. 1.

Avicenna. 1982. *Kitāb al-Najāt*. Edited by Majid Fakhry. Beirut: dār al-'āfāq al-jadīda.

Bychkov, Oleg. 2010. *Aesthetic Revelation: Reading Ancient and Medieval Texts after Hans Urs von Balthasar.* Washington: Catholic University of America Press.

Bychkov, Oleg. 2013. The Place of Aesthetics and the Arts in Medieval Franciscan Theology. In *Beyond the Text: Franciscan Art and the Construction of Religion*. Edited by Xavier Seubert and Oleg Bychkov. St. Bonaventure: Franciscan Institute Publications, pp. 196–209.

Bychkov, Oleg. 2014. 'But Everyone Experiences the Opposite': John Duns Scotus's Aesthetic Defense of Anselm's "Proof" of the Existence of God in Light of Present-day Thought. *Franciscan Studies* 72: 259–303. [CrossRef]

Bychkov, Oleg. 2015. "Metaphysics as Aesthetics": Aquinas' Metaphysics in Present-day Theological Aesthetics. *Modern Theology* 31: 147–78. [CrossRef]

Bychkov, Oleg. 2018. The Status of the Phenomenal Appearance of the Sensory in Fourteenth-century Franciscan Thought after Duns Scotus (Peter Aureol to Adam of Wodeham). *Franciscan Studies* 76: 267–85. [CrossRef]

Chatton, Walter. 1989. *Reportatio et Lectura super Sententias: Collatio ad Librum Primum et Prologus*. Edited by Joseph C. Wey. Toronto: Pontifical Institute of Mediaeval Studies.

Chatton, Walter. 2002. *Reportatio super Sententias*. Edited by Joseph C. Wey and Girard J. Etzkorn. Liber I, Distinctiones 1–9. Toronto: Pontifical Institute of Mediaeval Studies.

Costa, Paolo. 2011. A Secular Wonder. In *The Joy of Secularism: 11 Essays for How We Live Now*. Edited by George Levine. Princeton: Princeton UP, pp. 134–54.

Denifle, Heinrich, and Emile Châtelain, eds. 1889. *Chartularium Universitatis Parisiensis*. Paris: Delalain Bros, vol. 1.

Eagleman, David. 2011. *Incognito: The Secret Lives of the Brain*. Edinburgh, London, New York and Melbourne: Canongate Books.

Eagleman, David. 2017. *The Brain: The Story of You*. New York: Vintage Books.

Evdokimov, Paul. 1996. *The Art of the Icon: A Theology of Beauty*. Redondo Beach: Oakwood Publications.

Lachance, Paul, ed. 1993. *Angela of Foligno*. New York: Paulist Press.

Levine, George, ed. 2011. *The Joy of Secularism: 11 Essays for How We Live Now*. Princeton: Princeton UP.

Ockham, William. 1967. *Guillelmi de Ockham Scriptum in librum primum Sententiarum. Ordinatio*. Opera Theologica 1. Edited by Gedeon Gál and Stephen Brown. St. Bonaventure: The Franciscan Institute.

Olivi, Petrus Iohannis. 1924. *Quaestiones in Secundum Librum Sententiarum*. Edited by Bernhard Jansen. Quaracchi: Typographia Collegii S. Bonaventurae, vol. 2.

Perler, Dominik. 2001. What Are Intentional Objects? A Controversy Among Early Scotists. In *Ancient and Medieval Theories of Intentionality*, idem ed. Leiden, Boston and Köln: Brill, pp. 203–26.

Pinborg, Jan. 1980. Radulphus Brito on Universals. *Cahiers de L'Institut du Moyen-Âge grec et Latin* 35: 133–37.

Quenot, Michel. 1996. *The Icon: Window on the Kingdom*. Crestwood: St. Vladimir's Seminary Press.

Sendler, Egon. 1999. The Icon: Image of the Invisible. Elements of Theology, Aesthetics and Technique. Redondo Beach: Oakwood Publications.

Taylor, Charles. 2011. Disenchantment-Reenchantment. In *The Joy of Secularism: 11 Essays for How We Live Now*. Edited by George Levine. Princeton: Princeton UP, pp. 57–73.

Thompson, Nancy. 2016. The Franciscans and Stained Glass in Tuscany and Umbria. In *Mendicant Cultures in the Medieval and Early Modern World: Word, Deed, Image*. Edited by Sally J. Cornelison, Nirit Ben-Aryeh Debby and Peter Francis Howar. Turnhout: Brepols, pp. 22–44.

Vasalou, Sophia. 2015. *Wonder: A Grammar*. Albany: SUNY Press.

Warner, Michael, Jonathan VanAntwerpen, and Craig Calhoun, eds. 2010. *Varieties of Secularism in a Secular Age*. Cambridge: Harvard UP.

Willmott, Glenn. 2018. *Reading for Wonder: Ecology, Ethics, Enchantments*. Cham: Palgrave Macmillan.

Wodeham, Adam. 1990. *Lectura secunda in Librum Primum Sententiarum. Prologus et Distinctio Prima*. Edited by Rega Wood and Gedeon Gál. St. Bonaventure: St. Bonaventure University.

Article

'... With a Book in Your Hands': A Reflection on Imaging, Reading, Space, and Female Agency

Diane Apostolos-Cappadona

Catholic Studies Program, Georgetown University, Washington, DC 20057, USA; apostold@georgetown.edu

Received: 28 January 2019; Accepted: 6 March 2019; Published: 11 March 2019

Abstract: The Dutch artist, Johannes Vermeer (1632–1675), created a series of singular paintings that might be identified as feminine soliloquies of solitude, silence, and space. Like seeing, reading is a mediated practice that occurs within the cultural matrix that promotes the appropriate social mores of how to read, what to read, and who is able to read. Over the millennia of Western cultural history, books have been ambiguous symbols of power that have signified authorship, divine inspiration, wisdom, social position, and literacy. This led to the initiation of a singular Christian form of literature—the advice manual—specifically prepared for Christian women by Jerome (347–420), perhaps best known as one of the church fathers, translator of the Vulgate, and penitential saint. Simultaneously, an iconography of women reading evolved from these theological advisories, and paralleled the history of women's literacy, particularly within Western Christian culture. The dramatic division that has always existed between male readers and female readers was highlighted during the Reformation when Protestant artists recorded the historical reality that readers were predominantly men of all ages but only old women, that is, those women who were relieved form the duties of childbearing and housekeeping, and who, as a form of spiritual preparation for death, meditated upon the scriptures. The magisterial art historian Leo Steinberg documented the tradition of what he termed "engaged" readers in Western art. Engaged male readers dominated numerically over female readers as reading, Steinberg determined, was not a primary, or perhaps better said appropriate, activity for women. Yet Vermeer's portrayal of a young woman absorbed in textual engagement with a letter was an exquisitely nuanced visual immediacy of intimacy merging with reality that was highlighted by a refined light that illumined the soft, diffuse ambiance of this woman's world. How Vermeer was able to focus the viewer's attention on his female subject and her innermost thoughts as she is "lost in space" reading provides a starting point of this discussion of the images, reading, space, and female agency in Christian and in secular art.

Keywords: art; aesthetic; haptic; iconology; iconography; book(s); reading/readers; Jerome; Magdalene; Vermeer

---

An artist has contrived to lure me out of myself into an illusion of reality more fulfilling than any lived reality can be (Schjeldahl 2009).

1. Prolegomenon

This essay has been a journey of reflection, not simply of a favored motif in religious and secular art, but more personally with the re-emergence of several critical texts upon which much of my thinking has been developed over the years. Despite the scholarly vocation to be thorough both in research and in writing, every one of us stands upon the proverbial "shoulders of giants," and oftentimes we have so assimilated or reinterpreted their ideas we believe they have become our own. Given the diversity of my scholarly proclivities which are grounded in multi-disciplinary studies of religious art and cultural history with emphases on symbolism and on the iconology of women, I have come to stand on the shoulders of more giants than most of my colleagues. This reality became apparent as I worked through my thinking for this present text, despite the fact that my primary point of entrée was as usual a careful viewing of an image, in particular, Vermeer's painting of a woman reading.

Through this essay, readers will find references, both in my text and its footnotes, to several of those giants who have been with me, some simply through their books, others through personal encounters. None more significant for this present style of a reflection on a work of art and its effects upon a viewer than André Malraux[1] (1901–1976) whose own writings fused together the experience of art with the discriminating eye of a scholar. A writer who worked outside of the traditional boundaries of academic disciplines, Malraux gave us the vocabulary of the "museum without walls"[2] and of the significance of silence as a communicative mode for the observer engaged with a work of art.

Essential to this capacity for communication is composition, color, light, and form within the frame of the work of art.[3] This exchange can be identified as established through the aesthetic as the etymological foundation of this word is derived from the Greek αισθητικόσ. By providing an answer to the epistemological question of how we come to know—for we "come to know through the senses"—the aesthetic is more than an experience of or vision of the beautiful. The Greek root emphasizes the plurality of the human senses, not simply sight or touch, but all of the human senses uniting to transmit and/or to receive meaning and value.

---

[1] Perhaps better known today as a leader of the French Resistance during World War II, a political theorist, and novelist, André Malraux was an art theorist, publisher, and editor after the war. He served as the French Minister of State for Cultural Affairs from 1959 to 1969 and counted among the achievements of his tenure the restoration of historic buildings in Paris, the U.S. exhibition of Leonardo's *Mona Lisa*, the commission for the ceiling of the Paris Opera to Marc Chagall (1887–1985), and the establishment of the Maisons de la Culture throughout France. His first publication on art was his 3-volume work *La Psychologies de l'art* (1947–1949) which was translated into English with separate titles including *Museum without Walls* (1949) and *The Voices of Silence* (1951). It is interesting to note for this present study that among the four works of art reproduced on the cover of the 1973 Princeton University Press edition are details from two Vermeer paintings, *The Geographer* (c. 1668–1669: Städel Museum, Frankfurt) and *Girl with a Pearl Earring*. Malraux's later art publications include the 3-volume *Le Metamorphose des dieux* (1957), of which only the first volume was published in English as *Metamorphosis of the Gods* (1960). His work at the French publisher Gallimard included being the founder and director of the 30-volume *L'Universe des formes*, which was published in English as *The Arts of Mankind*. The impressive number and arrangement of illustrations which form a separate text on their own was one of the most striking characteristics of all of Malraux's art publications. This was appropriate given his understanding of "the imaginary museum," which allowed one to recognize the relationships between works of art as opposed to what Malraux perceived as the over-intellectualizing of art found in museums. He expressed concern that museum displays divorced art from its original function and thereby transformed its meaning, which can be seen as prophetic of the now contemporary interests in the study of reception and response, material culture, and visual culture, as opposed to the more traditional categories of art history that emphasized style and technique. Further, for Malraux, art was spiritually enriching and necessary for humanity, as evidenced by its capacity to transcend time through a process of metamorphosis.

[2] Looking across my desks and bookcases which are littered with museum postcards and clippings of works of art, I confess to being enormously relieved when I found those wonderful black-and-white photographs of Malraux standing, sitting, dancing, and resting on his side as he made both the selection of images and their arrangement for the first edition of his 3-volume publication *Le musée imaginaire de la sculpture mondiale* (1952–1954). His floor was littered with even more images than I could imagine placing around my office. How wonderful to realize I had taken unconsciously to creating my own "museum(s) without walls." For an academic study of Malraux's practice and his significance in the publication of heavily illustrated art books, see (Grasskamp 2016).

[3] I am using the term frame here not simply to signify the wooden or metal border that encases a work of art but also the space that the work of art dominates within and beyond the boundaries of that encasement. This understanding of frame is application to a sculpture as well as a painting.

Chief among the elements of form, especially in terms of the aesthetic dimension, is the human body, which expresses emotion and meaning through gesture, posture, position, and facial expression. Again, one of the key words associated with the human senses is haptic, which is derived from the Greek απτική, literally "sense of touch," which I suggest can be expanded to the "emotive physicality of the human body," especially in terms of the communicative potential of art (Apostolos-Cappadona 1992). My exploration of the haptic dimension of the human body in the arts was influenced by the psychologist and composer Louis Danz (1897–1977), who wrote in his psychological study of Picasso's art, "Picasso's line is like Martha Graham's dancing. Martha Graham, dances the path of feeling as it flows through her body. It flows through her body before it comes out."[4]

The artistic milieu that served as an additional support for this interpretation of the aesthetic and the haptic was established in the profound silence that both generates and inspires meditation and contemplation. However, this is not simply silence as an environment devoid of sound, but rather one empty of noise and dissonance. It is a realm of harmony and serenity that invites the observer into the quiet space manifested in a work of art and which allows for thought, reception, and response. This is as much as a sanctuary as it is a creative haven for introspection and spirituality. It is to paraphrase the feminist author Virginia Woolf (1882–1941) that "every woman needs a room of one's own" (Woolf 1929).

2. Women Reading in Vermeer's Paintings

Images of women are predicated upon the visual relationship between bodily gestures and postures as indicative of modes of action (or inaction). As the British economic historian and medievalist Eileen Powers (1889–1940) suggested, "the position of women is often considered as a test by which the civilization of a country may be judged" (Powers 1975). Definitions of gender are culturally and socially conditioned. Works of art are primary and fundamental evidence for understanding history, especially in terms of societal and theological values.

The Dutch artist, Johannes Vermeer (1632–1675), created a series of singular paintings that might be identified as feminine soliloquies of solitude, silence, and space. For example, his *Woman in Blue Reading a Letter* (c. 1663: Rijksmuseum, Amsterdam) (Figure 1) can be described as a visualization of poetic timelessness, and was possibly the inspiration for the 1999 best-selling novel *Girl in Hyacinth Blue* by Susan Vreeland (1946–2017). Her fictional narration of the history of an otherwise "lost" or imaginary Vermeer painting of a woman named Magdalena sewing quietly within the parameters of her own "space" and its multiple effects on the women who owned it throughout history affirms this reflection on the relationship between imaging, space, and female agency.

Vermeer's actual portrayal of a young women absorbed in textual engagement with a letter exquisitely nuanced visual immediacy of intimacy merging with reality that was highlighted by a refined light that illumined the soft, diffuse ambiance of these women's worlds. How Vermeer was able to focus the viewer's attention on his female subject and her innermost thoughts as she was "lost in space" reading provides a starting point for this discussion of the images of reading women in Christian and in secular art.

---

[4] (Danz 1974), see especially page 6. See also my abovementioned essay "The Essence of Agony," page 45 and note 3 on page 47.

Figure 1. Johannes Vermeer, *Woman in Blue Reading a Letter* (c.1663: Rijksmuseum, Amsterdam). On loan from the City of Amsterdam (A. van der Hoop Bequest). Courtesy of the Rijksmuseum, Amsterdam. SK-C-251.

3. Women Readers in Christian Art and Cultural History

Like *seeing*, reading is a mediated practice that occurs within the cultural matrix that promotes the appropriate social mores of how to read, what to read, and who is able to read. Over the millennia of Western cultural history, books have been ambiguous symbols of power that have signified authorship, divine inspiration, wisdom, social position, and literacy. Traditionally for Christians, books can lead one to or away from salvation. In earliest Christian art, books signified the Christian message and were only seen in the hands of men. The books of classical authors such as Ovid or Homer, or worse yet, Plato or Aristotle, were deemed to be harmful to the Christian life, should not be read, and were forbidden to women. Therefore, the average Christian, especially female Christians, needed guidance in order to discern the appropriate nature and subject of reading and of books.

This led to the inauguration of a singular Christian form of literature—the advice manual—specifically prepared for Christian women and initiated by Jerome (347–420), best known as one of the church fathers, translator of the *Vulgate*, and penitential saint. Given his proclivity to a male-dominated worldview, it is perhaps remarkable that Jerome advocated for female literacy as delineated in his "Letter to Eustochium: *The Virgin's Profession*" (Jerome 1933a) and in his "Letter to Laeta: *A Girl's Education*" (Jerome 1933b). It was for him an appropriate mode of Christian nurture as every mother should be able to read the Bible to her children. He compiled a careful reading list for Christian women. Similar advice manuals for women were authored by Christian theologians in the 15th and 16th centuries, particularly in Northern Europe, and again in the 19th century, especially in America.[5]

Simultaneously, an iconography of women reading evolved from these theological advisories, and paralleled the history of women's literacy within Western Christian culture. The dramatic division that has always existed between male readers and female readers was highlighted during the Reformation, when Protestant artists recorded the historical reality that readers were predominantly men of all ages, whereas only old women were depicted reading. Those women were relieved of the duties of childbearing and housekeeping, and thereby were "free" to meditate upon the scriptures as a form of spiritual preparation for death, such as those found in Gerard Dou's *Old Woman Reading a Lectionary* (1631–1632: Rijksmuseum, Amsterdam) or as a form of spiritual instruction by their husbands as depicted in Rembrandt's *The Mennonite Preacher Anslo and His Wife* (1641: Staatliche Museum, Berlin).

This iconography is both supported by our traditional assumptions about the Reformation as a literacy revolution, while questioning the presumption that only the upper classes, the elite, were literate. However, given what we believe to be the Protestant accent on literacy and the development of the moveable-type printing press, popular literacy could have become more of a reality from the 17th century forward. In principle, if not in fact, Protestantism advocated a literate laity who regularly studied the Bible as Dou's old woman and Anslo's wife did.

The magisterial art historian Leo Steinberg (1920–2011) documented the visual tradition of what he termed "engaged" readers in Western and secular art.[6] Engaged male readers dominated numerically over female readers as reading, Steinberg determined, was not a primary, or perhaps better said appropriate, activity for women. This was due in part because of society's then-accepted gender distinctions between men and women as it did with the symbolism of the book and the meaning of reading.

Jerome advocated for women's literacy, especially as a mode of Christian nurture for her children, and compiled a careful reading list for Christian women to follow throughout their lives. Among Jerome's letters to women are two long and famous treatises on *A Girl's Education* in *Epistola 107* addressed to Laeta, Paula's daughter-in-law and mother of her grandchild, Paila; and throughout the

---

[5] As an introduction to the development of advice manuals for women and the commensurate development of the iconography of women readers in 19th-century America, see (Apostolos-Cappadona 2002).

[6] The art historian Leo Steinberg proposed that women readers could be interrupted, i.e., the Virgin by the Archangel Gabriel, whereas men readers were protected from interruption by their wives or colleagues in his illustrated lecture, "Woman with Book, or The Interrupted Reading (How Men Perceived Female Readers from the 14th Century to Modern Advertising)," at Georgetown University in March 1985. His three paradigms for interrupted female readers were the Virgin Annunciate, the Penitent Magdalene in the Wilderness, and Francesca from Dante's *Divina Commedia*. The implications were clear to Steinberg that intellectual activity was secondary for women but primary for men. To my knowledge, this stimulating lecture was never published by Professor Steinberg.

lengthy text of *Epistola 128* to Gaudentius' daughter, Pacatila.[7] Both outlined educational programs that stressed an ascetic way of life and emphasized the importance of learning how to read and study Scripture. The letter to Laeta contained famous pedagogical advice; in other words, her education was designed to associate physical play, her bodily experiences, and her very identity of herself in history with her reading of Scripture. He considered education in letters much more essential for defining *who* a woman will be rather than for determining what she will *do*.

An effective and impassioned champion of women's rights to read Scripture, his practice of dedicating 12 of his surviving 23 biblical commentaries to women departed radically from his Jewish and Christian predecessors. For example, in his *Commentary on Zephaniah*, he inserts a long catalogue of heroic women drawn from the Hebrew Scriptures and from classical history.[8] His authority as a scriptural commentator and theologian began to establish a woman's right to read while being linked to his understanding of their greater spiritual needs due to their weaker nature.

Further, these varied actions on Jerome's part—especially his dedication of his texts to esteemed Christian women such as Paula, Eustochium, and others—had significance beyond the theological and the societal because it was neither deemed typical or appropriate to dedicate didactic works or serious religious literature to a lady. Thereby, Jerome departed from the customary ancient gift-giving or dedicatory practice in three meaningful ways: first, his willingness to instruct women in reading Scripture and learning what he considered to be the most important lesson in life, religious truth; second, in his preference for relationships and familial patterns based on spiritual rather than biological bonds; and third, in his confident assumption that the shared experience of reading and meditating on Scripture would create and renew these spiritual bonds linking himself, his chosen readers, and religious truth.

Reading, then, for Christian women was premised upon Jerome's advice to Demetrias, "Love to occupy your mind with the reading of scripture," especially as a mode of Christian nurture for her children.[9] Jerome's admonition provided both a meticulous reading list and emphasized the care which must be taken "with a book in your hands."[10] As both helpful and harmful, then, books played an ambiguous role in a Christian culture. Caution must be exerted as to who can create, control, hold, and **read** books.

By the early medieval period, the symbolism of the book, and thus, of reading, entered into depictions of the Virgin Mary at the Annunciation. Whereas, the tradition of Byzantine iconography of the Annunciation, by contrast, represented the Theotokos holding a spindle or being engaged in the act of weaving the royal purple followed the text of the *Protoevangelion of James*. This iconographic motif emphasized the visual analogies between the Annunciate Virgin and the virginal Athena who was the Greek goddess of wisdom and weaving.[11]

One of the early historians of women, Susan Groag Bell (1926–2015), studied the significance of medieval women book-owners as both commissioners and readers of books, particularly Books of

---

7   Jerome, "Letter 107 To Laeta '*A Girl's Education*'" as cited above in n. 4; and "Letter 128 To Gaudentius" are available in the *Christian Classics Ethereal Library* available online at http://www.ccel.org/ccel/schaff/npnf206.v.CXXVIII.html (accessed on 25 December 2018).

8   Consisting of three books of diverse letters to a variety of individuals written between 390 and 406, Jerome's *Commentary on Zephanion* is available in the *Libri Commentariorum, PL* 25 ed. Migne, 947-1578A.

9   Jerome, "Letter 130 To Demetrias" in *Jerome: The Principal Works of St. Jerome* ed. Philip Schaff (New York: Christian Literature Publishing Company, 1892) and reprinted as Volume VI of *A Select Library of the Nicene and Post-Nicene Fathers of the Christian Church, Second Series* ed. Philip Schaff and Henry Wace (Edinburgh: T&T Clarke), 444–461. Quoted passages from #7, page 451. Available online at http://www.ccel.org/ccel/schaff/npnf206.html (accessed on 25 December 2018).

10 Ibid.

11 The weaving of the royal purple and the weaving of the new life in Mary's womb were emphasized in the iconography of the Annunciation in the Eastern Orthodox tradition as metaphors for gestation; see Diane Apostolos-Cappadona, "Ömür/pli'ni Büken Kadinlar" ("'Mary took the true purple, and did spin it' .... Of spindles, looms, and women in Western art and culture") in *P+ Art and Culture Magazine* special Turkish-language thematic issue dedicated to *Tekstil ve Sanat (Textiles and Art)* 44 (2007): 106–16. Later issued as "Women Who Weaved the Thread of Life" in the English-language issue entitled "*Textile and Art*" of *P+ Art and Culture Magazine* 17 (Autumn 2008)): 60–76.

Hours and, more significantly, the interior illuminations.[12] Bell established the introduction of the book into the iconography of the Annunciation scenes as contemporary to the development of the illustrations for Books of Hours commissioned by these women as early as the 11th century and more commonly beginning in the 12th century. This new medieval image of the Annunciate Virgin with a book, Bell indicates, not only gave these medieval women a sacred role model, it allowed their literacy to exist—for if Mary read at this most singular of moments in human history *then* what medieval lady shouldn't learn to read in imitation of Mary?

By the High Renaissance, the image of the Virgin with a book was commonplace as evidenced by Raphael's *La belle jardinière* (1507: Musée du Louvre, Paris) and Vittore Carpaccio, *The Virgin Reading* (1510: National Gallery of Art, Washington, D.C.). Nonetheless, in both of these paintings of the Virgin with a book, it is exactly that—the Virgin *with* a book. Her attention is diverted from the act of reading, hers is as Steinberg has noted an interrupted reading. Women readers, he argued, through his three paradigms in western art of the Virgin Annunciate, the Magdalene in the Wilderness, and Francesca from Dante's *Divina Commedia*, were always interrupted by their domestic or marital (read sexual) duties, whereas male readers were protected from such interruptions by dutiful wives, mothers, or daughters. Therefore, women readers in Christian art, be they saints or sinners, were not exempt from interruptions as for example in depictions of Mary as a young mother rocking her son's cradle as she reads, for example, in Martin Schongauer's *The Holy Family* (c. 1480/1490: Kunsthistoriches, Vienna) or Rembrandt's *The Holy Family with Angels* (1645: Hermitage, St. Petersburg).[13]

In early Christian art, as noted earlier, the persons depicted with books were predominately, if not solely, men. As an emblem, the book became associated with a diversity of female saints and heroines in the early medieval period. Nonetheless, St. Anne—the mother of the Virgin Mary and the grandmother of Jesus—was represented as a model of the ideal mother who either read to her daughter and/or her grandson, or was engaged in the activity of teaching her daughter and/or her grandson to read. For according to the then-common understanding, mothers were responsible for the early education of children as wives were for the edification of their husbands. This imagery originates and is most popular in 14th/15th century northern European painting.

Similarly, the iconography of the popular female saint Mary Magdalene as a reader developed in the 15th-century work and was related directly to the development of popular literacy, the medieval understanding of reading, and the lay spirituality of the Devotio Moderna and the Brotherhood of the Common Life. Reading was understood to be simultaneously as a spiritual nourishment and as a physical act. Ideally, an audience should assimilate a devotional text enthusiastically and comprehensively

This Magdalene motif emerged in the medieval period as her gesture, pose, and costume designate that the introduction of the symbolism of the book, and therefore of literacy, signified more than emblematic usage. The first representation of the motif of the Magdalene as reader is found in the work of the Flemish artist, Rogier van der Weyden (1400–1464) in the altarpiece fragment of *The Magdalene Reading* (1436: The National Gallery, London).[14] Although the motif of a holy woman reading was not unknown by that date, there was no scriptural precedence for the Magdalene to be a reader as, similarly, there was no scriptural justification for the image of the Virgin Mary as a reader. Yet this

---

[12] (Bell 1982). Bell's now classic study remains pertinent as evidenced in the more recent studies of medieval women readers and iconographers by current medievalists and art historians, for example, see (Havens 2017); and (Smith 2003). An early advocate for the field of women's history, Bell recognized art as primary documentary evidence for historical study, see her "Discovering Women's History Through Art in the Classroom," *The History Teacher* 6.4 (1973): 503–510.

[13] Bell illustrated her earlier and now classic essay with two unusual illuminations which signify a qualification to Steinberg's thesis as these relate to the Virgin reading; however, not at the moment of the Annunciation, but rather in other episodes of the Nativity story. See Plate #1: Northern French Book of Hours, *The Virgin reads while Joseph rocks the swaddled Babe* (early 15th century: Walters Art Gallery, Baltimore), MS, 10.290, folio 69; and Plate #8: Flemish Book of Hours, *Virgin reading on the donkey, while Joseph carries the Babe on their Flight into Egypt* (1475: Bibliothèque Royale Albert Ier, Brussels) MS. IV 315, fol. 105v.

[14] (Apostolos-Cappadona 1997). Curiously, Vreeland's imaginary *Girl in Hyacinth Blue* was named Magdalena.

motif, of the reading Virgin, which began as we now know from Bell's research as early as the 12th century, flourished in the 14th and 15th centuries. Further Christian iconographic precedents were found in the iconographies of the virginal Saint Barbara and the scholarly Saint Catherine. So, one ponders why the motif of the reading Magdalene didn't originate earlier and why it began in the 15th century at all?

The simplest solution to the latter question is that either Rogier van der Weyden's patron's wife was named Magdalene or Madeline, or that his patron(s) requested the inclusion of this image within the context of the larger altarpiece from which this fragment survives. However, such assumptions are only that and are much too simplistic for an artist as theologically complex and iconographically original as Rogier van der Weyden. So, we must delve deeper both into his own invention of visual motifs, and the cultural and religious milieu of his world. In this process, this painting is not considered as a singular presentation or invention of an image but within the context of what the British scholar of the social history of art Michael Baxandall (1933–2008) identified as the "period eye."[15]

Recent studies in northern European art history have indicated two important factors for this study of the reading Magdalene. First of all is the central importance of individual Christian piety and devotionalism in the thematic presentations of 15th-century Flemish art. Although, northern art is often stereotyped as "cold" or "emotionless" in contrast to the more physically dynamic and passionate images of Italian art. However, the work of Rogier van der Weyden and his contemporaries communicated emotion and meaning through careful innovation in gesture and pose of the human body similar to my understanding of "the haptic." This style of painting, like the contemplation and meditation advocated by the Devotio Moderna, demanded the viewer's attention and required receptivity and response.

The northern European art historians Craig Harbison (1944–2018) and James H. Marrow (b. 1942) affirmed the extraordinary ties between Christian piety and devotionalism evidenced in 15th-century Flemish art (Marrow 1986; Harbison 1985). They saw this interconnection most clearly expressed by the artists who "found the means to visualize, subtly and fully, the chief religious ideal of the time, lay visions and meditations." The visual norm became the quiet, simplicity of a devout Christian meditating upon a text until the image of that text became visible within the frame of the painting. Many 15th-century Flemish paintings and manuscript illuminations depicted this exact moment, that is, of a reader who reads in the fullest medieval sense of the term. Following the then-common metaphor of the book as food the reader needed to masticate, swallow, digest, and, by digesting, assimilate the meaning of the text which was visually signified by an excretion of the crucial visualization of the *meaning* of the text. Thus, Rogier's *The Magdalene Reading* had both companions, and a religious and artistic context.

It was in fact this relationship between lay piety such as the Devotio Moderna and the rise of vernacular literature[16] that formed the cultural base for Rogier van der Weyden's *The Magdalene Reading*. Further, as Bell had promoted the importance of devotional texts such as Books of Hours for medieval women readers, more recent scholarship in medieval history has revealed among newly found records of medieval book ownership that devotional works were then most widely circulated among women. The purpose of these devotional books favored by women was within the guidelines established by Jerome to increase the religious fervor in the female reader and to instruct readers in the basic principles of the Christian faith.

Thus, the symbolism of women's literacy was affirmed through images of saintly women from the Virgin Mary, Saint Anne, Saint Mary Magdalene, and Saint Barbara, to Saint Catherine with books. As societal roles for women changed in the ensuing European cultures, the symbol of the book once

---

[15] (Baxandall 1988). Ironically, similar to Malraux's "imaginary museum" sought to recreate as the original context, function, and meaning of a work of art.

[16] By this time in western cultural history, Latin had become basically inaccessible to women as the contemporary educational practice identified it as a form of male puberty ritual.

again became a prop, an object which characterized one as a woman of social position and, perhaps, of some education. However, the exceptions are found in the work of Vermeer.

4. Vermeer's Women Readers: Reflections on Female Solitude and "Chinese Patience" in Secular Art[17]

Several centuries and transformed cultural contexts separate the visual evolution of women readers in medieval and Renaissance Christian art from their late 20th-century descendants in the art of the German painter Gerhard Richter (b. 1932) and the British photographer Tom Hunter (b. 1965). One of the foundations for the didactic authority of the visual image is its ability to repeat and reconstruct the commonly recognized masterpieces of earlier societies. Thus, an aura of both respectability and authority descended from one generation to another or from one cultural epoch to another.

While the motif of women readers has had an enduring presence in Western art, its evolution from a religious into a secular motif was bridged by the 17th-century Dutch artist Johannes Vermeer, whose oeuvre included his most celebrated *tronie*[18] known as *Girl with a Pearl Earring* (c. 1665: Mauritshuis, The Hague). Both Richter's *Reader* (1994: San Francisco Museum of Modern Art, San Francisco) and Hunter's *Woman Reading a Possession Order* (1998: Victoria and Albert Museum, London) reflect the restrained emotion and contemplative ambiance found in the earlier iconology of Christian women readers, while incorporating significant elements of Vermeer's works that focused the viewers' attention on an exquisitely nuanced female subject and her thoughts about the text in her hands within a balanced composition that was filled with a soft, diffused atmosphere.

Although the modern perspective of Vermeer is almost one of reverence given the quality of his painting, during his lifetime and into the 19th century he was neither so well known nor his art so immediately recognized as it now has become. A result of both his deliberate style of painting and his early death in 1675, Vermeer's oeuvre verges on the minimal. While as many as 60 or as few as 40 finished works may have survived into the 21st century, only 35 have been definitively attributed.

Little is known of his early life or his training as a painter. Less is known about his mature career as he had neither pupils or proteges, and the majority of his works were collected by a small circle of patrons in Delft. However, toward the end of the 19th century and early into the 20th, Vermeer's carefully balanced compositions and his painterly preoccupation with the behavior of light brought him to the attention of a wider public, especially following the May 1921 exhibition of Dutch painting featuring his *View of Delft* (1660: Mauritshuis, The Hague) and *Girl with a Pearl Earring* that was on view at the Galerie nationale du Jeu de Paume in Paris.

Marcel Proust (1871–1922) was then engaged in the writing of the sixth part (*The Captive*) of his multivolume literary masterpiece *À la recherche du temps perdu*. Published in several volumes between 1913 and 1927, Proust's reflection on the passage of life and of time included a discussion of over one hundred artists. However, it was the affect and effect of Vermeer's *View of Delft* as an apprehension of the approaching death of the elderly writer Bergotte that continue to engage the memory of many readers. Often understood as an autobiographical passage, if not a premonition of Proust's own last days, Bergotte's last excursion was to see a display of the Vermeer paintings. Remarkably stunned by the Dutch painter's art, Bergotte never ventured out again and remained apparently transfixed by the *"petit pan de mur jaune"*[19] in the *View of Delft* until his death.

---

[17] See note 19 below for a discussion about the significance of Vermeer's paintings for Marcel Proust.

[18] Derived from the 16th/17th century Dutch term for "face," a *tronie* was the representation of a common type of man or woman who were identified as an expression of an interesting character. However, a *tronie* was neither a portrait nor a depiction of an identifiable individual, rather, it was a "stock character" created either imaginatively or as a composite of generic human facial features and expressions.

[19] According to several Proust scholars, the author was entranced by Vermeer's paintings. "Ever since I saw the *View of Delft* in the museum at The Hague, I have known that I had seen the most beautiful painting in the world." (Watt 2013). Further,

No less dramatically, the British author Agatha Christie (1890–1976) had her perspicacious detective Hercule Poirot solve the murders of a brother and sister, and then identify an unknown Vermeer as the motive in her 1937 mystery *After the Funeral* (1937). When the painter Cora Lansquenet is savagely murdered several days after her brother's funeral, the family solicitor is concerned and calls upon his friend Poirot. The contents of the painter's home are to be sold at auction, including her paintings; however, her companion Miss Gilchrist is allowed to keep a painting. She carefully selects a work that fools everyone except for Poirot, who recognizes that there is something amiss when he learns that the scene is derived from a postcard not from life, as was the artist's inclination. He announces that the disguised painting which had been purchased at a jumble sale is in fact a Vermeer, had been painted over by Miss Gilchrist who recognized its value, and that the uncovered Vermeer would sell at auction for a sum that would have allowed Miss Gilchrist to return to her preferred life owning a tea shop.[20]

More recent authors, ironically both women, Tracy Chevalier (b. 1962) and Susan Vreeland (1946–2017) have also been inspired by Vermeer and expressly by his paintings of women. Chevalier credited her own decade-long fascination with a poster of Vermeer's painting for the development of her 1995 bestselling novel *Girl with a Pearl Earring*. This fictionalized narrative, which relates how Vermeer came to create a painting, was transformed into a 2003 film starring Colin Firth as Vermeer and Scarlet Johansson as the fictional household servant Griet.[21] The film was an eloquent adaptation of the novel's major interpretation of Vermeer as an artist of light, color, and silence.

Vreeland's 1999 novel was inspired not by her first-hand viewing of the extraordinary 1995 exhibition *Johannes Vermeer* at the National Gallery of Art in Washington but, rather, by her extended encounter with the exhibition catalogue.[22] While a spectacular presentation, the exhibition was made famous by the simple fact that it had been scheduled to be on view from November 12, 1995, through February 11, 1996, during the unpredictable and unprecedented lengthy shutdowns of the US Government, which resulted in the National Gallery of Art being closed from December 16, 1995 until January 6, 1996. Lines of disappointed foreign visitors who had planned their travel months in advance to see this exhibition became fodder for the international media and Vermeer's name was suddenly on everyone's lips.[23]

However, Vreeland's proverbially intimate encounter with Vermeer's paintings, especially his female subjects like *Girl Reading a Letter at an Open Window* (c. 1657–1659: Gemäldegalerie Alte Meister, Dresden), *Woman with a Pearl Necklace* (c. 1662–1665: Staatliche Museen, Gemäldegalerie, Berlin), and *Woman in Blue Reading a Letter*, came within the confines of her own domestic space. Thereby, Vreeland's fictional recitation of her imaginary Vermeer painting and its travels through multiple centuries and owners was perhaps created from her own firsthand experiences as a woman reader engaged by the delicate balance of the images and words found throughout the "book in [*sic.*] her hands."

Here we find what may be the critical elements to the appeal of both Vermeer's art and his women readers: the social projection of intimate encounters between a woman and a book within the solitude of her own domestic environment. This artist was a master in both the creation of innovative scenes

---

one of Proust's biographers, Edmund White, noted that "Indeed, on the night before he died, Proust dictated a last send, 'There is a Chinese patience in Vermeer's craft.'" See (White 1998).

20 Ironically, the most recent televised version of *After the Funeral*, starring David Suchet, transformed the Vermeer into a Rembrandt. Perhaps the financial value of a Rembrandt portrait was more recognizable by 21st-century television audience.

21 David Joss Buckley's 2008 play *Girl with a Pearl Earring* premiered at The Royal Haymarket Theatre in London. However, it was neither a success with audiences or critics, and to the best of my knowledge has not been re-staged since.

22 Ironically, Vreeland's description of her encounter with Vermeer and his works through the exhibition catalogue rather than the actual exhibition echoes Malraux's now classic dictum that "An art book is a museum without walls." See his *Museum without Walls* (London: Martin Secker & Warburg, Ltd., 1967).

23 The topic of many luncheon, dinner, and cocktail parties focused on whether anyone present had in fact seen the then now-elusive exhibition and, if they had, when did they see the Vermeer paintings and how did they get into the National Gallery of Art? In a curious twist of fate as I was revisioning this previous essay, the US Government had entered into a lengthy shutdown and the National Gallery of Art was once again closed to the public.

of everyday life and in imbuing them with emotional intensity. The interior of these homes can be characterized as expressions of an aura of privacy, comfort, and personal dignity. Predominately inhabited by women, either by the artist (or patron's) preference or simply because the domestic environment was then identified as a "woman's sphere," the majority of Vermeer's identifiable oeuvre can be described as soliloquies of female solitude.

His portrayals convey a magical immediacy as the viewer communes with the woman absorbed either in the act of reading or of writing a letter which the artist has subtly substituted for a book. By so doing, Vermeer has added a compelling emotion to the mystique of these paintings as any viewer recognizes the potential of a letter, especially one that demands intense scrutiny by its reader. So, the viewer empathetically wonders if this is a business transmittal, perhaps demanding an overdue payment, or is it more hopefully a love letter? If it is a *billet-doux*, then the viewer's curiosity is engaged as to the authorial possibilities—is it from a lover? a husband? a fiancée? or simply from a family member or friend?

This artist has succeeded, perhaps unintentionally, in creating not merely a work of art but a spatial narrative for the empathetic viewer. The gestures and postures of Vermeer's women readers (or writers) haptically conveyed an emotional intensity to the viewer and animate the domestic environment they occupy. If we consider his *Woman in Blue Reading a Letter* (Figure 1) as a normative example of Vermeer's reading (and even of his writing) women, we come to recognize a variety of visual elements that both reflect his careful study of the behavior of and the symbolic possibilities of light, the formal relationships between color and human emotions, and his compassionate empathy with his subjects.

As a painter, Vermeer was intensely preoccupied with imbuing each picture with the world he was creating by means of his methodical working style, time-intensive in detail, and discriminating in the relationships among color, light, and subject. Further, he coordinated his images through naturalistic effects and harmoniously balanced compositions. Thus, the visual subtleties within his pictorial frame were highlighted by the soft blur of the foreground and often also the background as the central figures, especially of his reading (and writing) women, were represented in exacting detail and precise focus. His careful observation of a vanishing point usually between the woman's face and the letter highlighted his central subject, like the woman reader dressed in a clear blue and mustard-yellow costume in *Woman in Blue Reading a Letter.* He further emphasized, at least for me, this reader's power of introspection as representative of her intellectual capacities, even *if* the text in her hands is a *billet-doux*. For she holds the letter with reverence and is engaged in an intense, if silent, dialogue with its author.

This artist's singular pattern of luminosity promotes the viewer's receptivity of this quiet and mysterious domestic ambience in a painting like *Woman in Blue Reading a Letter* without initially recognizing that this space is closed off from the larger world. Despite the exchange of light and shadow, within the painting's frame, there may be an implied window or an actual one as there are in other Vermeer's depictions of reading and writing women, for example, *Girl Reading a Letter at the Open Window* or *Lady Writing a Letter with Her Maid* (1670–1671: National Gallery of Ireland, Dublin), there is no exterior view to be seen, to complement the interior action, to identify the geographic location, or to provide a wider scope of "the real world." Without a recognition of the outside world, either of a landscape, architecture, or personages, Vermeer accentuates his female subject's privacy within her own enclosed space and thereby within her own narrative. Some scholars have commented that, in the works of Vermeer, this lack of an exterior view of the outside world indicated that such empty window is an obvious metaphor for engagement within this reader's (or writer's) interior world. This is the case, especially, for those interpreters with a religious or spiritual perspective who understand interiority as a projection of this woman's soul. Enclosure, then, is not imprisonment, but rather a private and intimate environment that permits the solitude and silence fundamental to contemplation and introspection. Thus, the viewer recognizes that this artist provides both his subject and his audience with that delicate balance of mind and body essential for intellectual and spiritual activity.

Thereby, these women readers exist within their own unique space as they are absorbed within into a private world of poetic timelessness. A painter of subtle enigmas, Vermeer represents his women readers (and writers) engaged with their epistolary communications. He emphasizes this by positioning them either in profile with their faces turned downward as they concentrated on their tasks, or with their backs toward the viewer. Whenever visible, their faces are not individualized like portraits so that the communicative focus is more abstracted as the viewer becomes mesmerized by the evocation of tranquil solitude. Without the malice of the male gaze, Vermeer transports the viewer into the aura of an awestruck voyeur who is invited to share in this woman's singular environment.

5. Coda Following Malraux: "To Love a Painting Is to Feel That This Presence . . . Is Not an Object but a Voice . . . "

Through this reflection on the world of women readers in Western art, we have traversed a road that the poet Robert Frost would have identified as *"the one less traveled"* (Frost 1916) through the forest of Christian cultural history, art theory, and the paintings of Vermeer. This matrix of influences and ideas have suggested an etymological retrieval of the meaning of the aesthetic as beyond a philosophy of the beautiful to a mode of knowing through the unified perception of all the human senses. Additionally, the term and meaning of haptic has been revived here to highlight not only the significance of the human body in works of art, but especially its fundamental ability to express meaning and value without words. These reformulations have informed this interpretation of Vermeer's presentations of women reading (and writing) and the response of women viewers to such visualizations.

However, there are further elements to consider as we conclude this journey, for clearly Vermeer possessed an artist's sensibility to empathize with the intimate psychology of individuals, so that his subjects were to paraphrase Malraux (n.d.) *"not simply an object but a subject."* The tenderness with which Vermeer rendered his women readers (and writers) reveals not simply his concern for them as subjects but also his sensitive attention to the uniqueness of their tasks. His reading (and writing) women present an ability for intellectual absorption, suggesting not only engagement with the import of the narrative but also with their potential for independent thought as they create their own world within and beyond that text. These women, then, are capable of psychological introspection given the moral and intellectual integrity they exhibit within their environment. From a late 20th- and 21st-century feminist perspective then, Vermeer's reading (and writing) women can be identified as a distinct category of women who signify both the significance of literacy and of independent thought.

Just as Virginia Woolf sounded the clarion call that "every woman needs a room of one's own," Vermeer has created a vision of how that woman's space could look. So, to paraphrase William Wordsworth, Vermeer, like Rogier van der Weyden, earlier Christian artists, and even Saint Jerome help us as *"we see into the life of women."* (Wordsworth 1798).

Funding: This research received no external funding.

Conflicts of Interest: The author declares no conflicts of interest.

References

Apostolos-Cappadona, Diane. 1992. The Essence of Agony: Grünewald's Influence on Picasso. *Artibus et Historiae* 13: 31–47. [CrossRef]

Apostolos-Cappadona, Diane. 1997. Picturing Devotion: Rogier's Saint Luke Drawing the Virgin and Child. In *Rogier van der Weyden's Saint Luke Drawing the Virgin and Child: Essays in Context*. Edited by Carol J. Purtle. Turnhout: Brepols, pp. 5–14.

Apostolos-Cappadona, Diane. 2002. *A Daughter's Own Book*: Women Readers in Antebellum America. *American Art Quarterly* 19: 8–13.

Baxandall, Michael. 1988. *Painting and Experience in Fifteenth-Century Italy: A Primer in the Social History of Pictures*. New York: Oxford University Press.

Bell, Susan Groag. 1982. Medieval Women Book Owners: Arbiters of Lay Piety and Ambassadors of Culture. *Signs* 17: 742–68. [CrossRef]

Danz, Louis. 1974. *Personal Revolution and Picasso*. New York: Haskell House. First published 1940.

Frost, Robert. 1916. The Road Not Taken. Available online: https://www.poetryfoundation.org/poems/44272/the-road-not-taken (accessed on 13 January 2019).

Grasskamp, Walter. 2016. *The Book on the Floor: André Malraux and the Imaginary Museum*. Los Angeles: Getty Publications.

Harbison, Craig. 1985. Visions and Meditations in Early Flemish Painting. *Simiolus: Netherlands Quarterly for the History of Art* 15: 87–118. [CrossRef]

Havens, Jill C. 2017. A Gift, a Mirror, a Memorial: The Psalter-Hours of Mary de Bohun. In *Medieval Women and Their Objects*. Edited by Jenny Adams and Nancy Mason Bradbury. Ann Arbor: University of Michigan Press.

Jerome, Saint. 1933a. Letter 22: To Eustochium: *'The Virgin's Profession'*. (dated 384). Available online: https://www-loebclassics-com.proxy.library.georgetown.edu/view/jerome-letters/1933/pb_LCL262.57.xml?mainRsKey=WJ2bsB&result=2&rskey=cewSfT (accessed on 24 December 2018).

Jerome, Saint. 1933b. Letter 107: To Laeta *'A Girl's Education'*. (dated 403). Available online: https://www-loebclassics-com.proxy.library.georgetown.edu/view/jerome-letters/1933/pb_LCL262.339.xml?rskey=JrVQyU&result=2&mainRsKey=0szd2e (accessed on 24 December 2018).

Malraux, André. n.d. Art Quotes. Available online: http://www.art-quotes.com/auth_search.php?authid=705#.XDzVuS2ZO-o (accessed on 31 December 2018).

Marrow, James H. 1986. Symbol and meaning in northern European art of the late middle ages and the early Renaissance. *Simiolus: Netherlands Quarterly for the History of Art* 16: 150–69. [CrossRef]

Powers, Eileen. 1975. *Medieval Women*. Cambridge: Cambridge University Press.

Schjeldahl, Peter. 2009. Dutch Touch: A Visiting Vermeer at the Met. *The New Yorker*, September 21. Available online: https://www.newyorker.com/magazine/2009/09/21/dutch-touch (accessed on 24 December 2018).

Smith, Kathryn A. 2003. *Art, Identity and Devotion in Fourteenth-Century England: Three Women and Their Books of Hours*. Toronto: University of Toronto Press.

Watt, Adam, ed. 2013. *Proust in Context*. Cambridge: Cambridge University Press, p. 84.

White, Edmund. 1998. *Marcel Proust: A Life*. New York: Viking/Penguin, p. 150.

Woolf, Virginia. 1929. *A Room of One's Own*. London: Hogarth Press.

Article

Beyond Making and Unmaking: Re-Envisioning Sacred Art

Daniel Gustafsson

Centre for Lifelong Learning, The University of York, Heslington, York YO10 5DD, UK;
dg.philokalia@gmail.com

Received: 16 December 2018; Accepted: 28 January 2019; Published: 31 January 2019

Abstract: This paper engages with predominantly Eastern Orthodox thinkers in reassessing the conditions under which sacred art may be possible today. The sacred has both ontological and cultural aspects. An artwork is sacred, firstly, by virtue of partaking of transcendent realities; and secondly, by being embedded in a worldview which allows the work to be made and received as sacred. Drawing on the thought of Philip Sherrard, the paper suggests that current conditions are characterised by cultural forgetting and the loss of such a metaphysical worldview. This paper proposes that the possibilities of sacred art must be rediscovered from within the practices of particular arts; and that this goes hand in hand with the rediscovery of a sacred ontology and of a Christian understanding of freedom. The paper will follow David Bentley Hart in affirming a theological understanding of freedom—as the orientation towards, and the attainment of communion with, ontological goods—against the prevalent postmodern and ultimately nihilistic notion of freedom as spontaneous volition. It is crucial, therefore, to also identify those transcendent goods towards which art may fruitfully be directed. In this light, the paper proposes the need to revise our concepts of matter, form, and, above all, beauty.

Keywords: sacred; art; freedom; beauty

---

1. Introduction

This paper engages with predominantly Eastern Orthodox thinkers in reassessing the conditions under which sacred art may be possible in the context of Western culture today.

The sacred has both ontological and cultural aspects. An artwork is sacred, firstly, by virtue of partaking of transcendent realities; and secondly, by also being embedded in a worldview and way of life which, by acknowledging those realities, allows the work to be made and received *as* sacred.

Drawing on the thought of Philip Sherrard, the paper suggests that current conditions are characterised both by cultural forgetting and the loss of such a metaphysical worldview. A change in the material conditions of art's production and reception cannot alone account for the crisis of sacred art; the change has happened also on the level of intellect and spirit. For this reason, any revival of sacred art cannot simply be a matter of contextual and material redistribution. What is needed is a genuine restoration or revision of our understanding of art and the sacred alike.

This paper proposes that the possibilities of sacred art must be rediscovered and reclaimed from *within* the practices of particular arts, and that this goes hand in hand with the rediscovery both of a sacred ontology and of a Christian understanding of freedom.

While, as Davor Džalto has shown, even postmodern conceptual art may stimulate fruitful theological reflection, not least on the nature of human freedom and creativity, it is important to consider whether such art has any ability to reorient our lives towards the sacred. Considering conflicting models of freedom, the paper will follow David Bentley Hart in affirming a theological understanding of freedom—as the orientation towards, and the attainment of communion with, ontological goods—against the prevalent postmodern and ultimately nihilistic notion of freedom as spontaneous volition. As long as both artists and audiences labour under postmodern notions of freedom, the paper argues, no sacred art is possible.

It is crucial, therefore, to also identify and credibly articulate those transcendent goods towards which the free creation of art may fruitfully be directed. In this light, the paper proposes the need to revise our concepts of matter, form, and, above all, beauty. The paper urges that we understand matter as both imbued with cultural meaning and as potentially spirit-bearing; that we understand form in terms of discipline and open-ended relation; and that we understand artistic beauty, not as immanent self-sufficiency or formal perfection, but as the manifestation of the divine gift.

Freedom can be understood in Christian terms as the freedom of the creature to flourish in the image and likeness of God; in this light, the paper suggests that also the free creation of an artwork—and the regenerative labour of artistic practice—attains its flourishing when it becomes in some manner iconic, sacramental, and theophanic.

2. The Possibilities of Sacred Art

Was music once a proof of God's existence?

As long as it admits things beyond measure,

That supposition stands. (Heaney 2015, p. 58)

Every artist implicitly affirms a world irreducible to its material parts. Any attempt to explain the arts in purely materialist terms, whether Marxist, evolutionary, or neurophysiological, entirely fails to do justice to the phenomenology—let alone the ontological implications—of both its creation and its reception.

"Creativity in the world is possible," claims Nicolai Berdyaev, "only because the world is created." (Berdyaev 2009, p. 129). The point is vital. Without a sense of the created world as having its origin in, and existing in relation to, the uncreated—without the world being open to, and dependent on, a reality that ontologically transcends and is other than the world—it is difficult to intelligibly entertain the possibility of human creativity as more or other than immanent procreation, re-creation, and re-organisation. "If there had not been a divine creative act," as Berdyaev argues, "in which something which had never been before was created, then the creative act in our world would be quite impossible." (Berdyaev 2009, p. 128).

If art is to have any ontological significance, we need a sense of human creativity as synergetic with the divine.

This would also mean that a sacred purpose and orientation is the true and natural mode of art; that art draws upon, and is directed towards, the uncreated source of all form, beauty, and being. Indeed, I will argue, not only that an ontology of participation, whereby the finite and material may partake of the spiritual and transcendent, is necessary to accommodate our great works of art, but that creative practice itself urges us to rediscover such an ontology from within the artistic traditions.

It is not necessary here to attempt a definition of sacred art; but it should be emphasised from the outset that sacred art is art that does not allow its audience to rest within, or retreat into, secular, materialist, or immanent models of explanation. In current circumstances, therefore, it is unsettling of prevailing notions. It is an art that asks us to revise our view of the world and reorient our lives towards transcendent goods—ultimately, towards God.

3. The Loss of Sacred Contexts

The making of art, if Berdyaev is right, is a cosmic event. It is also, of course, a cultural event. All art is contextual; it subsists and operates within specific conventions, practices, and shared understandings. This context is both cultural and ontological. It matters which worldview is assumed in the work's production and reception. These claims are perhaps especially true with respect to sacred art, not least the tradition of icon-painting. Pavel Florensky is emphatic: if you remove an icon from the liturgical, cultural, and ontological context of the Church, it ceases to be an icon.

Today, in a postsacral as well as postsecular world, we are rather in a situation where the church has, as it were, been removed from the icon. Intellectual and institutional bases for a sacred worldview are progressively dismantled or discredited. This loss of a sacred orientation in society would seem to result inevitably in the loss of sacred art. Such is the concern motivating Philip Sherrard in *The Sacred in Life and Art*. Sherrard was a poet, translator, and lay theologian. Disillusioned with the emotional, intellectual, and spiritual climate of the West, Sherrard's gradual conversion to Eastern Orthodoxy was sparked by his discovery of the poetry of George Seferis. In his admittedly rather sweeping analysis of the Western artistic tradition, Sherrard shows commonalities both with the Catholic artists Eric Gill and David Jones and with the Orthodox priest and scholar Pavel Florensky. For all these thinkers, artistic and spiritual decline go hand in hand. Thus, Florensky categorically claimed: "From the Renaissance on, the religious art of the West has been based upon esthetic delusion." (Florensky 1996, p. 67). In *The Sacred in Life and Art*, the culmination of Sherrard's reflections, he laments in particular the disastrous division between art and aesthetics, on the one hand, and metaphysics or theology on the other. First published in 1990, the book's diagnoses are arguably yet more acute today.

We should ask, with Sherrard, what power art possesses, in current circumstances, to resist a trend towards the all-encompassing desacralisation of human culture and conceptions. This is not simply a theoretical question. For the artist, it must also be answered in practice. Sherrard makes it clear that we must change our way of life. This should entail our way of *making* things as well as our way of doing things. At the same time, new action and new creation must be underpinned by new understanding. An art of genuine sacred orientation is needed; "yet given that an artist today would like to produce an art of this kind, is it possible for him to do so?" (Sherrard 2004, p. 36).

Sherrard stresses the all-pervading alienation that characterises our "mechanized, industrialized, dehumanized and desacralized world."[1] Art that is the product of such a world, that tacitly or openly affirms it, cannot alert us to—indeed, cannot but alienate us further from—the sacred. What, then, is the nature of art in such a world? What presuppositions govern its making and reception?

For Sherrard, these presuppositions are, broadly conceived, those of the humanist aesthetics championed by Herbert Read. The model derived from Read (if not always in line with his own vision) is art in relentless pursuit of originality; a pursuit which, untutored by the aesthetic, moral, and metaphysical ordering of goods, leads to increasingly arbitrary, wilful and transgressive expressions.

"The new—that which is innovatory—becomes a value in its own right," Sherrard explains, "and there can by definition be no authentic creativity without innovation, either in style or theme but preferably in both."[2] At the same time, since it is premised upon secular assumptions, "art and creativity cannot possess therefore any significance other than that which can be formulated quite adequately in hedonistic ('I know what I like'), sociological, scientific or psychological terms."[3]

In its stress on freedom from traditional forms, Read's model risks resulting in a lack of coherent continuity within the arts, inimical to the transmission, from one generation to the next, of both practical and theoretical wisdom. It also risks making any distinction between the creative and destructive, the vital and the vicious, all but impossible. "Ultimately," Sherrard comments, "art is to be regarded as the symbolic form of a specific, extended or heightened inner experience, though whether this experience is archetypal or merely the secretion of a morbid or corrupt subjectivity gone haywire it is impossible to assess."[4]

---

[1] Ibid., p. 4.
[2] Ibid., p. 52.
[3] Ibid., p. 53.
[4] Ibid., p. 46.

With no moral and metaphysical ordering, Sherrard argues, the ideas and images that govern the mental life of humanity "represent more and more an ontological perversion."[5] When such mental images "inform and animate" our art, "they produce not a revelation of the intrinsic sacredness of things, but a dislocation, a distortion that vilifies the very idea that life and art should be a bringing to birth of the beautiful and holy."[6] Artworks now help to perpetuate and vindicate a view of the world in which our alienation from transcendent and ontological goods is natural.

This is the crux of the matter: for much of modern and contemporary art, it has become not only the default position, but even the eagerly assumed mission of the artist to be, not a steward of the sacred, but an agent of desacralisation. The obstacle to any sacred revival in the arts, then, is not only entropic cultural amnesia, but a wilful negation of the perennial practical wisdom that has animated human making from classical times.

4. Theoretical and Practical Knowledge

A key assumption of Sherrard's is that the decline in art is precipitated by a loss or forgetfulness of traditional metaphysical awareness. He insists, thus, on theoretical knowledge as a "precondition of knowing in an experiental sense"[7]; and he argues that we must first reclaim a spiritual life before we can hope again to create a spiritual art. "Artists whose way of life does not include the experience of spiritual realities or even the acknowledgement of these realities," he maintains, "are simply deluding themselves when they talk of being in the front line in a cultural battle against [. . .] the vast inhumanity that typify our contemporary societies: they are the servants and victims and instruments of exactly the influences that have shaped these societies."[8]

We must be careful, nevertheless, not to suggest that the poem or painting is simply instrumental in the uttering or illustration of an antecedent proposition. Nor should we assume that any poetic treatment of sacred doctrine amounts to sacred poetry, or that any painting of a holy subject results in a holy painting.

There is a risk of Sherrard overestimating the role of antecedent knowledge, and so of underestimating the ability of artistic labour to, not only generate knowledge, but also constitute a mode of knowledge. The painter Ian McKeever's testimony is valuable here: "'In painting a painting one does not set out to paint what one knows, but rather tries to touch those things which one does not know and which perhaps cannot be known.'" (McKeever 2009, p. 24).

We should emphasise that, in the case of art, knowledge can and must be gained from *praxis* and participation. Any medium—poetry, painting, music—possesses a rich repository of practical wisdom that is only accessible through active immersion, as a result of keener discernment and increasingly refined modes of expression. It must be stressed, therefore, that our modern and postmodern forgetfulness is not only of the metaphysical, but also of the artistic, traditions: their roots, their resources, and their regenerative potentials.

It is important to challenge the pervasive assumption that artistic or authorial intentions are always antecedent to the creative act. In contrast, we can conceive of intentions as simultaneous with composition; as those of the sculptor who both moulds and manipulates his material and at the same time discovers the form his creation will take.

The assumption of antecedence can be disputed by the testimony of many authors and artists. Rowan Williams' comments on David Jones may suffice to indicate the importance of this type of experience: "the half-apprehended consonance of impressions out of which an artwork grows has to be realized in the process of actually creating significant forms which, in the process of their embodiment,

---

[5] Ibid., p. 14.
[6] Ibid., p. 15.
[7] Ibid., p. 131.
[8] Ibid., p. 34.

in stone, words, or pigment, uncover other resonances, so that what finally emerges is more than just a setting down of what was first grasped." (Williams 2005, p. 71).

It is in the dialogue between maker and medium—or perhaps between maker and the mystery of reality, as pursued through a particular medium—that the artwork becomes what it is, and that its unique meanings are realised. This experience is succinctly evoked by T.S. Eliot in *Little Gidding*:

> Either you had no purpose
>
> Or the purpose is beyond the end you figured
>
> And is altered in fulfilment. (Eliot 1944, p. 36)

5. The Postmodern Challenge

This has bearings, as we shall see, on how we think about the matter, form, and beauty of artworks. It also bears on certain tendencies of postmodern art, motivated as these are by a reaction against previous prevailing ideas of authorship and creative autonomy.

In light of the above examples, we can understand the pursuit of varying degrees of nonagency or unmaking in the artistic process. Davor Džalto, in *The Human Work of Art*, has admirably embraced the opportunity afforded by postmodernist art to reassess our conceptions of creativity, to move away from "modernist constructs of art and individuality [so as] to understand the very existence of the human being." (Džalto 2014, p. 103).

Yet the radical move towards nonagency may be motivated, at least in part, by overestimating the degree of autonomous agency in more traditional art. As the above examples indicate, and as further examples below will elucidate, the author or artist is less in control than is often assumed even in the case of traditional forms of art. Insofar as this is right, rather than jettisoning the practice of such art, the impetus should be to seek a deeper understanding of the implications of the synergetic nature of artistic creation.

Džalto, not unlike Sherrard, rightly observes that the modern notion of creative individuals, producing original works that bear marks of their unique "psychophysical characteristics and potential"[9] is problematic; for, "from a positivistic perspective, human creativity could be reduced to a complex web of various physical and chemical factors [which does not] represent any ontologically free activity of humans."[10] This last remark, however, should also serve to make us wary of the mechanisation and depersonalisation actively pursued by much postmodern art.

It is clear that postmodern art can make us think afresh about the production and consumption of art. For the purposes of this paper, however, the question must be asked: what power do these postmodern works have to reorient our vision towards the sacred and divine?

On Sherrard's assessment, even a poet like Gerard Manley Hopkins, for lack of a surrounding metaphysical culture, "cannot reveal to us that ours is a sacred universe" (Sherrard 2004, p. 146). What hope is there then for Warhol or Yves Klein? Are their works not too deeply embedded in the secular narrative to be able to show us a way out of it? Hopkins, arguably, can do more; at the very least, his verse should awaken us to the notion that perhaps ours is not an entirely desacralized universe. Further, Hopkins recommends a theological reading; indeed, his poetry requires a theological framework to yield its full meaning. More recently, the poetry of David Jones would seem to make similar demands. His masterpiece, *The Anathemata*, makes sense only within a sacramental ontology and therefore does something to show the value and validity of such an ontology.

The works of Warhol and Duchamp can raise questions about the nature of art and creativity, which in turn may engender theological answers, but there is nothing 'in' or 'about' these works themselves that urges us accept a sacred worldview. It is also fair to assume that a vanishingly small

---

9   Ibid., p. 50.
10   Ibid., p. 51.

section of the artworld (as of the general public) labours under theological conceptions. Indeed, while the changing nature of art appears amenable to Džalto's theological analysis, it is also the case that most of the theoretical and philosophical discourse accompanying this art appears resolutely anti-theological. There is in fact a tremendous risk that this change in art is received as a further move away from any need for a notion of the sacred.

An emphasis on automatic process, on ready-mades, on impulse and stream-of-consciousness—in short, any attempt to bypass conscious creative agency and embrace 'the death of the author'—can be seen to play into the hands of a mechanical and desacralised metaphysics. At the same time, a corollary trend can be seen; in a world vacated or inherent meanings, a new version of the arbitrary imposition of authorial subjectivity. This should urge us to consider the idea of freedom operative among artists, critics, and students of art today.

6. Models of Freedom

While a discussion of freedom is rather absent from Sherrard's analysis, it is central to Džalto's engagement with modern and contemporary art as well as to David Bentley Hart's diagnosis of modernity. Given its central importance in the contemporary cultural context, a consideration of freedom is relevant also for the purposes of this paper insofar as it bears on the issue of art and artistic practice.

It is right of Džalto, like Berdyaev, to affirm that our creative freedom is a mark and mode of the divine image in us; that we are beings "capable of creating, at least in some sense, out of nothing." (Džalto 2014, p. 33). We should indeed affirm that we create 'out of freedom', and not out of necessity; that our creation—both the act and the work—may therefore partake of the uncreated; and that something new therefore enters the world from beyond the finite. This means that the creative act itself gives the lie to the materialist presumptions of much contemporary art and theory.

It is equally vital, however, to maintain that our growth in the divine likeness is conditional upon the right and fruitful use of this creative freedom. Our freedom can be used creatively or destructively, to illumine and affirm those transcendent goods in which it has its origin and end, or to occlude and negate these. This vital point sets the pursuit of sacred art and life squarely against, not only the aesthetic, but the moral and metaphysical certitudes of modernity.

"We live in an age," writes David Bentley Hart, "whose chief moral value has been determined, by overwhelming consensus, to be the absolute liberty of personal volition"; and "any society that believes this must, at least implicitly, embrace and subtly advocate a very particular moral metaphysics: the unreality of any value higher than choice, or of any transcendent Good ordering desire towards a higher end." (Hart 2009, p. 1).

This is a nihilist metaphysics; because, as Hart makes clear, "For us to be as free as we possibly can be, there must be nothing transcendent of the will that might command it toward ends it does not choose or even fabricate for itself, no value higher than those the will imposes upon its world, no nature but what the will elects for itself." (Hart 2017, p. 314). This gives rise, in turn, to a nihilistic aesthetics, characterised by "explicit depictions of sex and violence" and "mindlessly brutal forms of entertainment" (Hart 2009, p. 77); by what Sherrard has already called "the search for increasingly violent forms of emotional or physical sensation." (Sherrard 2004, p. 34).

Crucially, Hart notes the initially theological origin of our current notion of freedom, as a product of late scholastic voluntarism and the reduction of God to pure power, before also claiming that it leads, almost inevitably, to atheism; "all genuinely *modern* stories of liberation, presuming as they do some version of this model of freedom, perhaps *must* terminate in a final rebellion against God: for he is the one intolerable rival who must be slain if humanity is ever truly to be free." (Hart 2017, p. 316). While the drama of this rebellion has been enacted in much modern art, perhaps most profoundly by Wagner, this model of freedom is inherently incommensurate with sacred art.

In this light, some further questions can be posed to the kind of art investigated by Džalto. For example, does Duchamp's practice of naming or renaming objects bring forth something essential or connatural to those object, or is it an arbitrary labelling? Does it not threaten, in that case, to subsume the labelled object under a voluntarist metaphysics? Rather than inviting us to celebrate the glory of the created and uncreated, do these practices tempt us with nihilism? Do they, in fact, suggest that the human will is the source of all value?

Conceptual art is problematic if the artist can decide, and needs to tell the unwitting audience, what a piece means. This legitimises again the so-called intentional fallacy, authorising the projection of a personal language. Meaning becomes something imposed by will upon inherently meaningless materials, rather than something emerging out of a responsiveness to those realities. Far from getting us away from authorial individualism, this aggravates it.

Conceptual art, then, can be seen to instantiate the same tendencies that Florensky identified in the particularly Protestant development of engraving: "the artistic freedom to arbitrarily choose the surface", the imposition by "the supposedly Pure Reason" of its "graphic schemata of reality [...] on materials that have nothing in common with them"; a destructive rather than creative activity, because "in exercising its freedom of self-determination, it violates the self-determination of the world; while, in proclaiming its own law, it thinks it unnecessary to attend to that law whereby all things in creation become authentically real." (Florensky 1996, pp. 111–12).

We risk, in short, ending up with a kind of voluntarism of the artworld, epitomised by the phrase 'it is art because I say so'. Instead, we want to be able to say something like this: it is art because, responsive to the revelatory and regenerative potentials of a given medium, it participates in the act of Creation; because, as C.A. Tsakiridou may say, it makes a thing or an aesthetic object that in itself hypostasises being.

For this to be possible, we need another ontological picture that can also harbour another realisation of freedom. The alternative model, most succinctly formulated by Hart, is this: "We are not free because we can choose, but only when we have chosen well." (Hart 2009, p. 79). On this classical and Christian understanding,

> true freedom is the realization of a complex nature in its proper ends, both natural and supernatural; it is the power of a thing to flourish, to become ever more fully what it is. But to think of freedom thus, one must believe not only that we possess an actual nature, but also that there is a transcendent Good toward which that nature is oriented. To be fully free is to be joined to that end for which our natures were originally framed, and whatever separates us from that end—including even our own personal choices—is a form of bondage." (Hart 2017, p. 313)

Hart stresses "that only a society ordered towards the transcendental structure of being—towards, that is, the true, the good, and the beautiful—is capable of anything we might meaningfully describe as civilization, as it is only in the interval between the good and the desire wakened by it that the greatest cultural achievements are possible." (Hart 2009, p. 90).

The need for a teleological, as opposed to a voluntarist, understanding of freedom was recognised also by Berdyaev. The latter, Berdyaev calls "childish, slavish freedom." (Berdyaev 2009, p. 290). Its nihilistic implications are evident: "Negative freedom, freedom as arbitrary free will, is freedom without content and void. To desire freedom for its own sake, freedom without purpose or content, is to desire emptiness, to turn away towards non-being." (Berdyaev 2009, p. 147). "A mature freedom," on the other hand, "a freedom with real content, predicates the maturing and uplifting of the inner man"; such freedom "has cosmic content and intention towards the world's goal: it is the opposite of wilfulness." (Berdyaev 2009, pp. 290–91).

Such freedom is the freedom of creation and regeneration; it is the freedom required for, and realised in, sacred art. Voluntarist freedom, meanwhile, is inherently iconoclastic. We see it in the incessant defacement, defecation, and desecration in contemporary art. As Roger Scruton notes, "It is not merely that artists, directors, musicians and others connected with the arts are in flight from beauty. There is a desire to spoil beauty, in acts of aesthetic iconoclasm." (Scruton 2009, pp. 173–74).

Sherrard is quite right, therefore, to say that religious or metaphysical concerns are far from irrelevant to the practice of art: "Art, like life, has one range of possibilities and purposes when you recognize and try to live in accordance with beliefs of a religious nature and quite another when you do not." (Sherrard 2004, p. 47) To put it bluntly, if we dispose of our traditional icons and replace them with sheep cut in half and canvases covered in shit, what does this do to our sense of who we are and can be?

Hart argues that modern freedom ultimately is "incompatible with a Christian view of the human being." (Hart 2017, p. 322). Arguably, so is much of modern and contemporary art. I suggest that insofar as art labours under such an idea of freedom, it cannot produce sacred works. Any sacred art must be situated within a metaphysics capable of accommodating a classical Christian model of freedom.

7. Matter and Meaning

The only way to escape alienation and desecration in theory, and the only chance of overcoming these in practice, is to have recourse to a theological ontology of participation. We need, as Hart and Sherrard as well as Džalto prescribe, a vision of the created as partaking of, and abiding within, the uncreated. Any genuine pursuit of sacred art today must operate within such an ontology. Crucially, such an apprehension of reality is implied by and enshrined within the artistic traditions. To discover the true potentials of art is to discover the only worldview in which such art is possible: an ontology which allows us to affirm the sacred potential, not only of the form and beauty of our art, but also of its very materiality.

Sherrard, giving his working definition of the sacred, notes: "We are at once in the midst of things. The sacred is something in which the Divine is present or which is charged with divine energies." (Sherrard 2004, p. 1). It is vital to stress that the created work or thing does not merely signify, but indeed partakes of, the uncreated or divine; so that this work itself is irreducible to its material 'thingness', because it is what it is only in relation to that which transcends it. This is at bottom, of course, a sacramental and iconic understanding of reality. On this understanding, the very corporeality of an artwork is integral, not antithetical, to its potentially spiritual aspects.

We know, not least from our experiences of art, that material things can be both mind-changing and spirit-bearing. The 'dematerialization' embraced by much postmodern art can therefore be challenged in light of what Andrew Louth, with Sergei Bulgakov, calls 'Christian materialism'. Already in John Damascene's defence of icons, of course, a vindication of sacred art entails an emphatic vindication of matter. Such a vindication is crucial for the sacramental, in art no less than in liturgy. As Louth reaffirms, "matter is God's creation; it is not to be despised; it is precious; it is capable of disclosing to us the creative power of the God who created it. It is only because we are material beings that we can participate in God in the Eucharist, a privilege denied to purely spiritual beings such as angels." (Louth 2013, pp. 113–14).

Matter can bear the countenance of divine beauty. All sacred art, in some manner and measure, rests on this assumption. Thus, even a contemporary painter like McKeever can both stress the materiality of his artworks and affirm their ambition to manifest a more-than-material light. "'A painting should light from inside itself,'" he claims. "'You should feel the emanation of light. I do not want to depict light but to have the painting giving light.'" (McKeever 2002, p. 12). This hope should be heard within the context of an ontology in which genuine transfiguration is possible. McKeever's paintings themselves, which are both elemental and angelic, testify to the possibility of matter becoming transparent to spirit.

What constitutes the matter of art is not, of course, straightforward. The example of poetry highlights both the ambiguity of this concept and its vital importance. Poetic artefacts are of an elusively nonmaterial kind; but they do rely on the 'matter', broadly construed, of the culture and language in which they operate. As both the practice and theory of David Jones make clear, every artist, whether visual, literary or other, relies upon handed-down cultural deposits no less than the raw materials of a medium.

Poetry certainly depends for its meanings on shared languages, both of the poetic tradition and of the wider culture, themselves conditioned by previous acts and artefacts of meaning-making. Given this human history, we may say that poetic matter itself is articulate. This relates back to the idea of creativity as discovery, of intention as in some sense synonymous with, rather than antecedent to, the act of making something in a particular medium. A classic evocation of this insight is given in Pasternak's *Doctor Zhivago* when the poet-physician experiences "what is known as inspiration":

> The primacy no longer belongs to man and the state of his soul, for which he seeks expression, but to the language in which he wants to express it. Language, the homeland and receptacle of beauty and meaning, itself begins to think and speak for man and turns wholly into music, not in terms of external, audible sounds, but in terms of the swiftness and power of its inner flow. Then [...] flowing speech itself, by the force of its own laws, on its way, in passing, creates metre and rhyme and thousands of other forms and constructions, still more important, but as yet unrecognised, unconsidered, unnamed. (Pasternak 2011, p. 390)

Matter and medium are themselves wellsprings of meaning, potentially charged with spirit. Language is not a lifeless instrument, nor some blank slate for arbitrary impressions and impositions; so far from being wilfully made to mean whatever a particular speaker wants it to mean, language itself is the prime mover, and the poet its mouthpiece.

We should not underestimate the extent to which a shared language must exist also for conceptual art to 'come off' as successful works or events at all. The conceptual artist, no less than the painter or poet, manipulates a repository of accessible meaning-charged 'matter'; in this case, the conceptual baggage of the history of art itself, as well the expectations of its contemporary practitioners and public. Insofar as any artwork attempts to realise its autonomy from shared meanings, we should worry about its ability, simply put, to be meaningful. One aim of art should be, arguably, to achieve enduring forms of meaning that can also sustain meaningful forms of life.

8. Form

We see in the excerpt from Pasternak the importance also of form, broadly conceived, as indispensable to creative fruition. Now, to appeal to the importance of form is not to endorse 'old' metres, manners, and methods (whether in poetry, painting or other arts), but to insist on the making of a 'thing' that has both integrity and allusive power; a thing that 'comes alive' as what it is, within the given parameters of its particular medium, while also existing in dynamic relations to other works and realities.

It was a repeated dictum of David Jones' that to make two marks is at the same time to make a third; namely, the relation between the other two. It is this invisible third mark which is the source of aesthetic value and meaning within the work, which grants the work its 'significant form' (to borrow a phrase from Fry and Bell). We may speak, with Tsakiridou, of an "aesthetic object" constituted by "dynamic relationships" of "aesthetic elements such as line, hue, tonality, texture, saturation, shape, form, etc." (Tsakiridou 2013, p. 117).

A commitment to form is crucial on a sacramental worldview. Art is implicated in a sacramental ontology by realising, as Jones puts it, the re-presentation of one thing or reality 'under the form' of another. So that a form, thus understood, is neither a self-sufficient entity nor the immanent closure of meaning, but, on the contrary, a mode of radical openness to an overabundant reality. A work receives its coherence and articulacy, therefore, not only through its internal dynamics, but also through relations to realities outside itself, in the sense of both a cultural and an ontological context.

For the contemporary Greek painter and iconographer, George Kordis, the "lines, colours, movements, etc." of an artwork are all understood as "energies" which "must be reconciled and exist in a [...] balanced dynamic state." At the same time, his "painting aims at creating an embracement between the object and the spectator." As such, it both "depicts" and realises a relation between the object and the subject. For Kordis, ultimately, the artwork may thus serve to realise a "state of love", "where the boundaries are lost, and life is an eternal communion." (Kordis 2019). This is an artistic and spiritual vision both in tune with the Orthodox tradition and sensitive to the problems and possibilities of a particular artistic medium in contemporary practice.

Form is not simply a prior constraint, arbitrarily imposed on artistic activity, but a framework emerging as a result of responsiveness to (and within) a particular medium; to (and within) a material culture; to (and within) a spiritual reality. An artwork subsists in a network of analogies.

As the example of Doctor Zhivago shows, when creativity is realised as responsiveness, form and freedom go hand in hand. An artist is, above all, a steward of meaning. He realises his own freedom, and the work itself achieves its liberty from the arbitrary, precisely in the service of, and communion with, transcendent goods. Art, therefore, makes virtually self-evident the idea that genuine freedom is possible only through constraints. The implications for art of Hart's proposed model of freedom is also clear from this argument:

> The form, as Michelangelo used to say, is liberated from the marble. In this way, precisely through accepting freely the constraints of a larger social and moral tradition and community, one gives shape to a character that can endure from moment to moment, rather than dissolving in each instant into whichever new inclination of appetite or curiosity rises up within one. One ceases to be governed by caprice, or to be the slave of one's own liberty. (Hart 2009, p. 79)

The creative life is more than analogous to the religious life, as the examples of the greatest religious artists and poets testify. It must be the aim of art both to redeem matter and to redeem the will; hence, the importance of following something analogous to a 'rule'; in the sense of answerability, not servility, to standards beyond the self. We can therefore understand form also in terms of discipline. Thus, for example, the use of metrical forms may in itself constitute a kind of ascetic practice.

"For an artist working within a religious perspective," as Sherrard explains, "the forms and images of his art are not his own discovery or invention: they are pre-determined, both on the plane of the imagination and correspondingly in the given canonical prescriptions of his particular religious tradition." He clarifies that "this does not signify that all an artist has to do is slavishly to copy the canonically prescribed forms: such a procedure would at once condemn his art to lifelessness and make it merely academic." (Sherrard 2004, p. 49). Nor, vitally, should a metaphysical or theological framework be imposed upon an artwork, but rather emerge from within it. This is the experience and testimony also of some key modern artists. Pärt's musical reorientation is, like John Tavener's explorations in the same medium, indissolubly artistic and spiritual. To discover the artistic potentials of a medium or a form *is* to discover its metaphysical implications, and vice versa.

It is through creative practice that an artist may, as it were, test the truth of certain metaphysical or theological propositions. So, McKeever, through profound and painstaking meditations in and on the medium of painting, tests the truth of the claim—embodied in the icon-tradition—that 'all is from light'. The meaning of this insight or outlook can only be assessed and articulated through the act of painting itself. The worldview in question will only be accepted as valid, by artist and audience alike, if it can be shown to bear creative fruit. We accept the notion that all being springs from and aspires towards the light if, and only if, we see that movement, and that light, manifested in the work of art.

9. Beauty

If we expect an artwork to reorient our desire and will towards God, what in the work itself can help us to do this if not, most emphatically, its beauty? It is right to challenge notions of immanent formal perfection, as well as notions of the individual artist as the source of all value in a work. Beauty, crucially, should not be understood either in formalist or subjectivist terms.

Taking our cue again from Berdyaev, there is a difference between sacred pagan and Christian art. For us, now, in the light of Hart's diagnosis of a world faced with the option of 'Christ or Nothing', we must affirm a sacred art that is Christian rather than pagan in its ontological and aesthetic commitments.

"In classic pagan art," Berdyaev argues, "there is an immanent completeness, an immanent perfection. Classically beautiful pagan art strives for finality and perfection of form here on earth, in this world." (Berdyaev 2009, p. 227). "In the art of the Christian world," however, Berdyaev continues, "there is not, nor can there be, a classic finality of form, immanent perfection [...] In this world only a striving towards the beauty of another world is possible, only the longing for that beauty. The Christian world permits of no closing-in, no finality in this world."[11] The critique of formal and final beauty as incompatible with Christian and theophanic art has also been levelled by C.A. Tsakiridou. Rowan Williams, meanwhile, has written in similar terms about the open-ended fiction of Dostoevsky.

Christian art should be responsive, indeed answerable, both to a historical irruption of liberty and inspiration, and to a pre-existing plenitude of form and beauty that cannot be contained within an immanent frame. The beauty here envisioned is a beauty of which the artwork may partake but not circumscribe or exhaust. In a Christian ontology of participation, a finite work of art may manifest what Hart calls the beauty of the infinite.

We should not expect Christian art, therefore, to strive for formal perfection, but perhaps rather to be elliptical, ecstatic, and epiphanic. Even brokenness, emptiness and silence—as heard, for example, in the music of Pärt—may inform a Christian artwork, the radical openness of which is what allows it to be held up to, and so to harbour and host in return, the uncreated.

We see in McKeever, again, how the forms of his paintings retain a diaphanous fluidity and translucency, in order to intimate rather than imprison an elusive presence. McKeever speaks of the painting emerging out of the relation between his own body and the body of the physical canvas before him. Faced with a blank canvas, he works *through* abstraction, not towards figuration, but towards form and presence. "'It is,'" he says, "'as if I'm trying to sense an image that is on the other side abstraction and moving away from the abstract rather than towards it.'" (McKeever 2009, p. 24).

Pertinent here is Tsakiridou's understanding of theophanic icons as simultaneously 'kenotic' and 'plerotic', self-emptying and spirit-filled: "Implicit is a movement towards the dissolution and augmentation of form, towards contraction and expansion consistent with the inexhaustible plenitude and withdrawal of the divine presence." (Tsakiridou 2013, p. 251). A theophanic artwork, whatever the medium, thus has an openness in its form, "in order to reveal in ever incomplete moments of being a deeper ground from where an elusive fullness arises."[12] We may perhaps speak of 'forms of irruption'; not the deliberate dissolution that characterises so much modern and contemporary art, but forms that manage to reintroduce, into the fragmented fabric of reality, a manifestation of transcendent plenitude.

More than aesthetic, beauty should be understood as a truly ontological manifestation. We can only ever analogously speak of beauty as a visible quality, for example, in poetic, musical, or conceptual works—perhaps, indeed, even in visual works. We can more lucidly and inclusively speak—in the words of David Bentley Hart—of "a handing over and return of the riches of being." (Hart 2003).

Irreducible to formal properties, no less than to dictates of will, this beauty is a gift. It is not created by the human artist. Nor is it simply added to a work after its formal completion, but is always already there as that towards which, within which, and at the prompting of which the artist works. The task of the artist is to peel back the layers of opacity which cover it, using the tools of his medium.

This is the opposite of a voluntarist account of beauty as wilful and subjective. "The beautiful is not a fiction of desire," Hart shows, "nor is its nature exhausted by a phenomenology of pleasure; it can be recognised in despite of desire, or as that toward which desire must be cultivated."[13] We may say the same of creativity. Beauty should be the aim and tutor of our creativity no less than our

---

[11] Ibid., p. 228.
[12] Ibid., p. 317.
[13] Ibid., p. 17.

desire: so that, within the particular practices of our chosen vocation, we can cultivate a closer and more articulate responsiveness to its real prompting and presence.

The artist needs to 'let beauty happen' and needs discernment to do so. Indeed, it takes skill also to know when and how to allow the gratuitous to take place, to become part of the artistic process and method. If this is true already of traditional practices, it is perhaps especially pertinent for artists that incorporate randomness and nonagency into their works. We can speak of a kind of ontological, not simply aesthetic, responsiveness to the manifestation of irreducible being itself in a particular medium or context.

Any sacred art, any art truly partaking of a sacred reality, is a product of divine–human cooperation. There is no surer sign of this synergy than the artwork's beauty. If we accept a sacred ontology, we cannot but accept beauty as one of its manifestations; and so we cannot but affirm beauty (properly understood as the splendour of being) as one of the aims of art. Sadly, Sherrard suggests, such beauty is "totally rejected by the activities of the secular world and most of what passes for its art." (Sherrard 2004, pp. 20–21). Nevertheless, or rather because of this, we must be committed to it. For it is beauty, above all, that allows us to rediscover a sacred ontology in the midst of a materialist world; not through theoretical study, but through direct experience of the irreducible.

10. Conclusions

In secular and postsecular times, the arts must increasingly vindicate a worldview which makes their own practices intelligible, let alone meaningful. Philosophy and theology have a supporting role to play here, to establish the conditions under which an artwork may be received as sacred, but the rediscovery of a committed artistic-spiritual discipline—of creative discipleship—is primary.

Sherrard rightly urges us to "heal the breach between art and metaphysics."[14] What is demanded, he suggests, is a kind of renunciation; a withdrawal from the superficially cultural battle in order to rediscover "that spiritual capital of which the art and life of our post-medieval world have been first the exploitation, then the dissipation, and finally the exhaustion."[15]

The challenge remains, however, to create art that is meaningful and intelligible here and now. Cultural knowledge will inevitably be subject to entropy. Regardless of this, or because of it, the artist must always find new ways of enabling communion between past and present, as well as between the created and uncreated. Any art with sacred ambitions must, in some manner and measure, become incarnate in the prevalent, postsacral and postsecular culture, even in order to leaven that culture with realities it has exiled and occluded.

Crucially, a metaphysical worldview should not be presented to the audience as an intellectual hypothesis. If an artwork is to be capable of granting an experience of existential and ontological re-orientation, then the work cannot simply be the expression of an antecedent proposition. We cannot expect readers, listeners, or viewers to accept a worldview that is not borne out, not embodied, by the artworks themselves. We need to withdraw into, in order to draw from, not only into the metaphysical but also the artistic traditions, their mediums and materials. We need to rethink originality as faithfulness to the origins (and therefore ends) of art. "We can and must go to the fount of things, can and must make all things new."[16]

It may indeed be that the more we come to understand, for example, what poetic language and poetic form are truly capable of, the more we may also grasp the potentials of our own creative humanity. To trace poetic art to its first principles and utterances is to arrive at mythopoeia, at prophecy, at prayer and praise; it is to arrive where aesthetics and metaphysics are indeed indissoluble. To trace

---

14 Ibid., p. 157.
15 Ibid., p. 35.
16 Ibid., p. 156.

visual art back to its first principles is to become ever deeper involved in a world in which sacramental re-presentation and new creation are possible.

The aim of art (of sacred art in particular) should be, as also C.A. Tsakiridou argues, to articulate and embody life. Tsakiridou singles out Rothko as a painter in whose work "representation becomes irrelevant" "because it is not 'art' anymore" but "has become a living reality." (Tsakiridou 2013, p. 276). Among contemporary visual artists, Ian McKeever is exemplary in his exploration—significantly inspired by the icon-tradition—of what painting is and can be.

Much is at stake. For we find ourselves in the midst of a conflict, not only of cultural values, but of ontological conceptions and commitments. Thus, Kordis seeks to address and assuage "the needs of contemporary people [who are] tortured by the void of relationships and the abyss of darkness." (Kordis 2019). McKeever, meanwhile, claims that a painter paints either towards the darkness or towards the light. This is true, of all the arts, in more senses than one. The aim of contemporary and future makers must be to choose the latter course: to pursue creative work as the revelatory and regenerative participation in an ontology of light.

Funding: This research received no external funding.

Conflicts of Interest: The authors declare no conflict of interest.

References

Berdyaev, Nikolai. 2009. *The Meaning of the Creative Act.* Translated by Boris Jakim. San Rafael: Semantron Press.

Džalto, Davor. 2014. *The Human Work of Art.* Yonkers: SVS Press.

Eliot, Thomas Stearns. 1944. *The Four Quartets.* London: Faber & Faber.

Florensky, Pavel Aleksandrovich. 1996. *Iconostasis.* Translated by Donald Sheehan, and Olga Andrejev. Crestwood: SVS Press.

Hart, David Bentley. 2003. *The Beauty of the Infinite.* Grand Rapids: Eerdmans.

Hart, David Bentley. 2009. *In the Aftermath.* Grand Rapids: Eerdmans.

Hart, David Bentley. 2017. *The Hidden and the Manifest.* Grand Rapids: Eerdmans.

Heaney, Seamus. 2015. *New Selected Poems.* London: Faber & Faber.

Kordis, George. 2019. My Painting. Available online: http://kordis.gallery/about/ (accessed on 18 January 2019).

Louth, Vladimir. 2013. *Introducing Orthodox Theology.* London: SPCK.

McKeever, Ian. 2002. *William Blake's 'Jerusalem', the Emanation of the Giant Albion.* London: Alan Cristea Gallery.

McKeever, Ian. 2009. *Paintings.* Edited by Marjorie Allthorpe-Guyton, Michael Tucker and Catherine Lampert. Farnham: Lund Humphries.

Pasternak, Boris. 2011. *Doctor Zhivago.* Translated by Richard Pevear, and Larissa Volokhonsky. London: Vintage.

Scruton, Roger. 2009. *Beauty.* Oxford: Oxford University Press.

Sherrard, Philip. 2004. *The Sacred in Art and Life.* Limni: Denise Harvey.

Tsakiridou, Cornelia A. 2013. *Icons in Time, Persons in Eternity.* Farnham: Ashgate.

Williams, Rowan. 2005. *Grace and Necessity.* London: Continuum.

Article

Contemporary *Misticism*: Recovering Sensible Aesthetics in an Age of Digital Production

Randall K. Van Schepen

School of Architecture, Art and Historic Preservation, Roger Williams University, One Old Ferry Road, Bristol, RI 02809, USA; rvanschepen@rwu.edu

Received: 28 January 2019; Accepted: 6 March 2019; Published: 12 March 2019

Abstract: Materialist accounts of artistic development emphasize the ongoing revolution of media in the progress of history. Amongst the most popular accounts of modernity are Walter Benjamin's essays on the relationship of photography to traditional art. His account of the loss of aura has been subject to countless reinterpretations since its publication. The present essay addresses the contemporary production of a number of architects and artists whose work provides an interesting challenge to the Benjaminian account of the secularization of artistic ritual. The artists Adam Fuss, Vera Lutter, Alison Rossiter, Sally Mann, and others have recently been exploring photographic methods that contradict the Benjaminian account of the history of photography. They continue to explore techniques that Benjamin placed in the auratic pre-paper-print era, such as Daguerreotypes and photograms, as well as employing other more material/chemically based effects. Such artistic choices are often considered nothing more than a nostalgic reverie trying to stem the tide of materialist history, a flawed search for a lost aura of presence. However, when these works are set against the backdrop of contemporary digitized production and of the Dusseldorf School as well as most other contemporary photographers, these "retro" works stand as a critical counterpoint to our present seamless digital imperium. The soft and hazy effects of these works, what I am calling their *misticism*, occludes the particularity of digital bits of information in a search to connect to the material and the sensual, something denied by information-saturated technologies. Even within a materialist approach to history, there is room to view these architectural and artistic effects as critically productive rather than merely retrograde. The present essay argues for the timely relevance of contemporary retro-photographic techniques in fostering both a critical attitude and as evidence of attempts to recover a sense of spiritual presence.

Keywords: aura; retro-avant-garde; aesthetics; mysticism; digital imagery; photography

---

Wilson: "But what shall we dream of when everything becomes visible?"

Virilio: "We will dream of being blind."

Paul Virilio, 1994[1]

1. Introduction: The Digital Imperium and *Mistical* Artists

Marching to an unknown future, present technologies of image production and consumption ceaselessly advance to ever greater levels of visual acuity. The digitized realm of experience we now float in has only made the striving for atomized clarity more obvious and more subject to the demands of an insatiable audience, on the one hand, and to the corporate and administrative purposes who

---

[1] Paul Virilio in Louise Wilson's interview (Wilson and Virilio 1994), "Cyberwar, God and Television: Interview with Paul Virilio." on *CTheory.org*, published 1 December 1994; accessed 1 December 2018 at http://www.ctheory.net/articles.aspx?id=62.

Religions **2019**, *10*, 186; doi:10.3390/rel10030186

www.mdpi.com/journal/religions

control its flow. Considered merely as a digital version of the historical string of ever-improving image-making technologies since the advent of photography, such restless strivings could be correctly understood as merely the latest manifestation of a pathetic, mindless, and reflexive industrial impulse beating at the heart of modernity—a desire to protect market share by constantly repopulating the commercial sphere with improved products that make last year's technologies at the very least unfashionable, if not functionally obsolete. It seems, however, that there is more at stake in our embrace of this endless, visually stupefying digital "progress" than such a structural economic analysis might reveal. The present essay suggests that such hyper-real digital imagery colonizes the material reality it points to, transforming our experience of materiality into one that is increasingly abstracted from the body. In response to this culturally dominant impulse, it suggests that certain architects and artists "mistify" images by occluding them in order to recover a more immediate and sensuous relation to the world, one that nevertheless also ushers in the spiritual.[2]

Carried along by this wave of innovation and digitized evolution, our consumerist environment is saturated with image-making and image-circulating modes of aesthetic production. The artworld is not immune to these larger tendencies. There is ample evidence of artists working in modes that take advantage of the qualities foregrounded in digitized production, whether through photography, video, virtual reality or other digitally immersive media. As Paul Virilio noted some two decades ago, "We cannot help but notice today the decline of ... *analogue* mental processes, in favor of instrumental, *digital* procedures ... " alienating us from the world to which it refers, a process which he traces back to Walter Benjamin's comments on print photography as "opening a field in which all intimacy yields to the illumination of detail.[3] This striking incompatibility between obsessive details and intimacy is explored here in relation to a sampling of recent works of art and architecture, whose ambiguous and indistinct character seems a conscious antithetical foil for the dominant desire for greater digitized clarity. The choice of such archaic imagery or techniques, leading to more ambiguous experiences, seems to invite an analysis of the metaphysical implications of such effects rather than a simple accounting for their merely sensually evocative character. The larger social context, of the seemingly inevitable subsumption of reality by the digital or the virtual will hover over this discussion much as the digital "cloud" hover over, above and beyond our direct experience or control. The implication of such artistic choices is that they come with metaphysical as well as sensual implications. Virilio suggests that the "endocolonization" of our lives by digital recording devices has the potential to lead to a "world without intimacy"—a "world which has become alien and obscene, entirely given over to information technologies and the over-exposure of detail."[4] In fact, Virilio argues that the level of this digital virtuality is so pronounced that is goes well beyond Jean Baudrillard's notion of *simulation* into a state of *substitution*. In Virilio's state of substitution, the digital realm is so powerful and prevalent as to be independent of the "original" reality to which it once might have referred. Thus, two realities exist instead of a singular reality to which the (digital) signifier points.[5]

Against this endocolonization, or at least in response to it, the artists and architects discussed here produce effects contrary to those typical of digitized bytes of visual information. The danger of the purely visual and wholly digitized data-body, Vivian Sobchack argues, is in its "devaluing [of] the physically lived body and the concrete materiality of the world" to the point that this "dominant cultural and techno-logic informing our contemporary electronic 'presence'" runs the risk of making

---

[2] The present study is related to similar research on affective, sensory, and bodily responses in aesthetic and political theory. For a summary of these haptic approaches in relation to architecture, see (Paterson 2016). His survey of the literature is oriented around movement in architectural experience more than bodily presence, but they are clearly related responses to a static vision organizing visual information.

[3] (Virilio [1998] 2000, p. 2). Virilio is referring to Benjamin's 1936 essay on mechanical reproduction (Benjamin [1936] 1992).

[4] (Virilio [1998] 2000, p. 57).

[5] (Wilson and Virilio 1994, interview).

us "merely ghosts in the machine".[6] The photographers Adam Fuss, Vera Lutter, Sally Mann, and Alison Rossiter and the sculptor Olafur Eliasson and architects Diller + Scofidio variously blur, occlude or obscure visual detail or information using mist, smoky, hazy or out-of-focus effects. This list is only a sampling of artists whose work employs occluded imagery or ambiguously articulated space. Others might include Gerhard Richter (photopaintings), Paul Graham (American Night series 2010–11), and Nina Canell's *Perpetuum Mobile* (2009–2010), to name a few. Because the techniques these artists and architects employ vary from the antique to the highly technological, this essay is not a diatribe against all things digital—although it must be said that the inherent strengths of a medium come into play as tendencies in production and reception. There is no avoiding the fact that the differences between digital and analogue photography, for example, are of such a magnitude that they press towards the likelihood of certain artistic choices being made, such as highly saturated color and obsessively plotted detail and resolution.

2. *Mistical* and Mystical

A final introductory note on the word "mysticism" versus my use of the term *misticism* in defining this creative strategy. The use of *misticism* firstly relates to the blurry and cloudy visual effect of these artists and architects. The fact that I have chosen architects and photographers as my main examples is also intentional, as both of these fields of cultural production foreground relations to the material world in a way that painting does not. When employing "misty" effects, they thus provide particularly problematic but also interesting test cases for the aesthetic under discussion. The major secondary association for the term *misticism* is, of course, in relation to theological "mysticism". Mysticism's association with via negativa is perhaps the most pregnant association for these *mistical* artists, as it is through the lack of information, the negated status of the image, that one comes to know the nature of the subject. This dialectical inversion of materiality into spiritual effect, of lack of information into presence, is the operational nature of these evocative rather than descriptive *mistical* works. The first thorough discussion of the cloudlike architecture of Diller + Scofidio's *Blur Building* in relation to *The Cloud of Knowing* is by Jeffrey Kosky.[7] In a very convincing and compelling analysis to which I am indebted, Kosky discusses a few contemporary artists who explore spiritual themes in their work. In a more aesthetically particular fashion, the present essay proposes that *mistical* effects are particularly effective at evoking the contemporary spiritual experience; ironically, they do so through a greater attention to bodily experience.

3. *Mistical* Spatial Articulation

Because the issues of spatial articulation are distinct from two-dimensional representation, initially I would like to introduce two sculptors and architects dealing with misty/foggy spatial articulations. Olafur Eliasson has worked on this kind of color- and mist-saturated space since the mid-2000s, with at least one of these works being constructed in collaboration with an architect. In 2003, Eliasson was chosen as the artist to take over the Turbine Hall of the Tate Modern, installing one of the most successful interventions in that series, *Weather Project*. 2009 and 2010 were especially productive years continuing this vein of exploration, with works such as *Your Atmospheric Colour Atlas* (2009) and *Feelings*

---

[6] Vivian Sobchack's idea of an ethical cinema that engages the "haptic" body can be found in her (2004) *Carnal Thoughts: Embodiment and Moving Image Culture*. (Sobchack 2004, p. 162). See also Laura U. Marks's notion of the (implied) element of touch in moving images, in (Marks 2008, pp. 399–407). Noting that film and video "become more haptic as they die", caused by scratches, fading and deterioration, Marks clarifies that her "definition of visual tactility, however, has little to do with physical texture and mainly to do with the way the eye is compelled to 'touch' an object . . . The techniques . . . do not necessarily make a film look tactile. However, optical printing can build up many layers of images on the film, producing a thicket of barely legible images" (p. 401). With obvious similarities to the artists and architects discussed here, she notes that filmic "graininess certainly produces a tactile quality, as the eye may choose between concentrating on figures and ignoring the points that make them up or bracketing the figures and dissolving among the points" (p. 402). Marks's theories are more fully developed in her *The Skin of the Film: Intercultural Cinema, Embodiment, and the Senses* (Marks 2000).

[7] (Kosky 2013).

Are Facts (2010), *Your Blind Movement* (2010), and *Your Blind Passenger* (2010) employing colored lights and a fog machine to create a highly saturated and indistinct spatial experience. Even in 2016, Eliasson produced *Fog Assembly* as a part of his intervention at the palace of Versailles. In addition to Eliasson's gallery interventions, an interesting and highly technical example of the construction of *mistical* space in architecture can be found in Diller + Scofidio's *Blur Building*, which was built for the Swiss Expo at Lake Neuchatel in 2002.

Eliasson's *Weather Project*, an immense warm-toned light installation in that vast hall, brought sun to London, hence its popularity. It was composed of a semicircular screen that radiated solar-colored light, a ceiling that was mirrored to encourage self-reflection and communal posing, and a gallery whose air was diffused with an artificially produced mist. Laying prostrate on the floor, lounging with one another, Londoners found the installation not only immensely rewarding physiologically, but also socially, as this gathering space fostered the organization of spontaneous social units, often made of participant bodies posing in shapes or words (a peace sign, the words, "Bush Go Home," etc.). Extending this popular if not critical success, Eliasson worked on a series of similarly atmospheric light installations in 2009–2010, beginning with *Your Atmospheric Colour Atlas*, which employed artificially produced fog infused with red, green and blue colored light (the additive colors of RGB) from a grid of fluorescent fixtures installed on the ceiling. Visually navigating these works became increasingly complicated as later pieces, such as *Feelings are Facts* with architect Ma Yansong, which was installed in the Ullens Center for Contemporary Art in 2010, changed the pitch of the floor from one end of the gallery to another along with dropping in the height of the ceiling grid. Participants therefore had to give up visually dominated navigation in order to adapt to this constantly changing spatial environment.

In each installation of 2009/2010, but especially with *Feelings are Facts*, viewers had to "constantly renegotiate their balance by shifting their weight and posture—with only the fields of colour to guide them intuitively through the dense atmosphere."[8] In the lack of distinction between participant and work, body and color, mist and solids, Eliasson's *mistical* works encourage a bodily processing of information in a way which is sympathetic to a phenomenological mode of understanding. Merleau-Ponty's notion of space as co-existent with the body rather than objectively separate from it (filling it as spatialized or spatializing rather than a mutually dependent relation) develops into a chiasmic sense of the exchange possible between the body and things. Choi (2014) has fruitfully introduced Elizabeth Stöker's notion of "attuned space" into his discussion of Eliasson. Eliasson's ambiguous spatial articulations seem to illustrate Stöker's attuned space as "not primarily an object for a subject who performs acts of spatial understanding. Rather, as attuned space, it has an appropriate mode of coexistence with the corporeal subject."[9]

There is an open question as to whether Eliasson's work participates in the construction of a society of spectacle. Spectacle, the definition of which has not achieved critical consensus, resides at the intersection of late capitalist corporate branding, seductive aesthetics, and an uncritically immersive experience.[10] It is against the sheen of seamless, highly produced, enticing aesthetic pabulum that contemporary critical artistic practice is set. Boris Groys, for example, suggests that "art must be directed against contemplation, against spectatorship, against passivity of the masses paralyzed by the spectacle of modern life."[11] While Eliasson's work has sometimes been critiqued as participating in the production of Debordian spectacles, these works construct experiences that are slow, meditative, and draw out sensual content not easily conformed to spectacle's purposes. Eliasson and the other artists

---

[8] Eliasson's studio's official website, https://olafureliasson.net/archive/artwork/WEK100050/feelings-are-facts (accessed on 12 December 2018).

[9] (Elizabeth 1965, p. 20).

[10] See Claire Bishop's critique of participatory practices, "Participation and Spectacle: Where Are We Now?" in (Thompson 2012, pp. 34–45). See pages 35–36 for her discussion of "spectacle."

[11] Groys in Bishop, p. 36; from Boris Groys, "Comrades of Time," *e-Flux Journal*, 11 December 2009, available at www.e-flux.com.

under discussion here employ effects that encourage what Renee van de Wall calls "tasten denken" in Dutch, or a groping form of thinking through the senses.[12]

Diller and Scofidio claim that the indistinct character of *Blur Building* (2002) and the viewer's inability to construct a coherent whole while experiencing it creates an environment that counteracts the contemporary desire for slickly-packaged and branded spectacle, even suggesting that it should be understood as "anti-spectacle". *Blur Building*'s mist-saturated, ambiguously articulated space shares a visual syntax of vague form, palpable atmosphere, and quieting softness with Eliasson's *Weather Project* and other foggy projects. *Blur Building*'s 90 by 70 m cage-like structure of pipes was suspended on a platform above Lake Neuchatel and emitted fine particles of water that created a cloud. This mist-cloud hovered above the water, enveloping the frame and participants, questioning the very nature of architectural enclosure—spatial enclosure being one of architecture's supposedly essential qualities. Figures walking through the mist visually appear and disappear, hovering on the edge of a felt rather than optically plotted presence. As Diller + Scofidio describe it:

> Upon entering the fog mass, visual and acoustic references are erased, leaving only an optical "white-out" and the "white-noise" of pulsing nozzles. Blur is an anti-spectacle. Contrary to immersive environments that strive for high-definition visual fidelity with ever-greater technical virtuosity, Blur is decidedly low-definition: there is nothing to see but our dependence on vision itself.[13]

Participants struggling with basic ocular recognition were given "brain coats" which were programmed with their personal preferences and which would light up when in the proximity of someone with similar tastes. *Blur Building*, like the Relational Aesthetics to which it is indebted, attempts to overcome the isolation of our postmodern age of information overload by fostering the emergence of a new *sensus communis*, but one that nevertheless acknowledges our present distance from each other.[14]

One of the most astute analyses of *Blur Building* was undertaken by Jeffery Kosky in *Arts of Wonder: Enchanting Secularity—Walter DeMaria, Diller + Scofidio, James Turrell, Andy Goldsworthy* (2013), a work that the present discussion has great sympathy with. Embracing Ashley Schafer's notion of *"inefficient* technologies," Kosky contrasts the Cartesian notion of illuminating things clearly and distinctly so that they are available for our rational mastery to Diller + Scofidio's project which is consciously designed to obfuscate any readily available rational understanding through its shrouded, cloaked, and ever-variable form.[15] Made in 2002, when the idea of the computational digital cloud was in its infancy, *Blur Building* nevertheless speaks to the contemporary, ambiguously formed digital identities we have floating in the cloud as well as the digital communities that are formed as a result. At the same time, the direct spatial experience forces an improvisational and intuitive response to its constant sensual reconfiguration, one that is subject to wind, light, participants, and unknown variables that "do not offer ultimate security, certainty or control".[16]

---

[12] (van de Wall 2008, p. 5): "'Tastend denken' then might describe a kind of thinking that is modelled upon the sense of touch as it is usually conceived: a thinking that has to make do without the overview accorded to sight, fragmentary and uncertain about its direction, but in close contact with what it thinks about and even assuming the form of what it holds."

[13] Diller + Scofidio on their website, accessed, 18 May 2011: http://www.dillerscofidio.com/blur.html. YouTube Video: http://www.youtube.com/watch?v=0WT5Lu1MKYs&feature=player_embedded#at=220.If out-of-focus-ness and blurriness are relatively common in works of two-dimensional art, they are decidedly not readily employed in the realm of architecture. Diller, Scofidio + Renfro have since changed their website and this quote is no longer a part of their description therein: https://dsrny.com/project/blur-building (accessed on 1 March 2019).

[14] The original formulation of "relational aesthetics" was introduced in 1998 by is Nicholas Bourriaud in *Relational Aesthetics*, les presses du réel: Dijon, 1998/2002.

[15] (Kosky 2013, pp. 69, 84).

[16] (Kosky 2013, p. 176).

4. Photography's Technological Burden

The creative fascination with clouds, blur, mist, fog, and other occluding visual effects is not limited to sculpture and architecture. If anything, drawing, painting, and photography are more likely to manifest these characteristics than the three-dimensional arts (which have to undertake heroic, often highly technical, efforts to *mistify* their forms). The shift from three- to two-dimensional imagery also requires a conceptual reorientation because not all two-dimensional media have an equally conflicted relationship between clarity and cloudiness, resolution and refraction, or definition and diffuseness. In the hands of the great Romantic painters, such as Caspar David Friedrich, the representation of mist is a way to evoke, among other things, the divine mysteries of nature. In drawing, the subtle, shrouded, tonal ranges of a George Seurat or Käthe Kollwitz's charcoal show the figure's gradual emergence out of a range of gray and black, without the defining linear marks that make up more typically defined drafted forms. In these cases, the blurriness of forms is not considered a compromise or denial of information but an embrace of the positive effects of fog or tonal subtlety. The painter Gerhard Richter discusses the "blurriness" of his out-of-focus photopaintings as a positive effect rather than a deficient image missing information. He defiantly claims that one cannot blur a painting, only a photograph. It is the presumed coherence and clarity of the photographic source image that is undermined by the haziness of its resolution. Ironically, Richter's claim notwithstanding, I would argue that this is the very reason why Richter's photopaintings *can* legitimately be called blurred. It is because Richter's photopaintings inherit the mantle of the presumed photographic clarity and indexicality of their source while denying it in paint. That is, we know that while Richter's source images were originally focused and that they also had a direct correspondence to the material reality that they representationally point to, he then proceeds to artistically destroy this relationship by occluding the image with his painterly effects. Other than examples such as Richter's photographically derived paintings, however, it is in contemporary photography more so than painting that one finds a strategic embrace of the veiled imagery characterized above as contemporary *misticism*. However, most photographic production proceeds in lockstep with the impulses that determine our present technological digital imperium.

The Dusseldorf School (Andreas Gursky, Thomas Struth, Candida Höfer, Thomas Ruff, etc.) represent an approach to photography that has led to large-scale, digitally produced, informational-laden images flooding into contemporary galleries. Following on the heels of their more conceptually oriented teachers, Bernd and Hilla Becher, Dusseldorf school photographers adapted their anonymous, factual images to the newly available digital technologies, increasing the size, resolution, and intensity of color of the Becher's multiple-image *Typologies* series. However, instead of a wry wit employed in the chronicling of vernacular architectural forms, Dusseldorf photographers chose highly saturated spectacular images that impress with a massive display of discrete bits of visual data. Although Dusseldorf School photographs and the images of those who follow them exist at such a scale as to dwarf the viewer, virtually enveloping them, the feeling is less of a sensual surrounding than of an undifferentiated field of discrete bits of information, information for the eye rather than experience available for the body.

This pursuit of a more seeming fidelity in the "big digital photograph" directly mirrors the same trajectory of consumer image-technologies, from VHS to DVD to Blu-ray to HiDef to 4K to VR. The relentless megapixel race is currently running up against our ability to even discern differences between 1080/HD, 2K, 4K/UltraHD, 8K, etc. These resolutions present images so vibrant that they promise to sate our desire to see imagery at a level of definition that rivals or even supersedes that of life. As participatory practices in performance art seek direct contact with the audience/participant, consumers are simultaneously being enveloped in and shaped by the virtual spaces we navigate between on the screens distributed throughout our daily existence: From tablet, to computer, to projector, to TV.

Ironically, as screens increase in size and are more fluidly integrated throughout life, continually pulling us into the vortex of isolated digital experience, we are abdicating the social and political sphere in which avant-garde practice is supposed to operate. How is it that we can recover a sense of the body in this datascape? Vivian Sobchack suggests that a sense of embodiment is necessary to counteract, or to simply act, in the face of the constant digitization of life. Ethical recovery is discovered through the body, where "the lived sense and feeling of the human body [is] not merely as a material object one possesses and analyses among other objects but as a material subject that experiences and feels its own subjectivity."[17] Thus, even though artistic production should be in step with technological progress, technology should provide an opportunity to recover our ethical bodily presence and not merely reiterate the cultural logic that produced the technology. As Adorno warns, "the growing relevance of technology in artworks must not become a motive for subordinating them to that type of reason that produced technology and finds its continuation in it."[18]

5. *Mistical* Contemporary Photography

It is against the contemporary atmosphere of the reigning digital imperium—further enabled, I would suggest, by the work of many contemporary digital photographers—that the "retro" effects or techniques of Fuss, Derges, and even Ruff is best understood. Instead of a mere romanticizing of contemporary life, the ambiguously misty and occluded forms they construct can be understood as attempts to reengage the contemporary body with materiality. Rexer's term, the "antiquarian-avant-garde",[19] is appropriate for artists such as Sally Mann, Fuss, and Derges who employ 19th-century photographic techniques such as photograms and Daguerreotypes to produce some of their imagery. However, ambiguous images that call forth a more embodied form of consumption can also be produced by more technological means, such as those found in the work of Thomas Ruff or Alison Rossiter, both of which harness media to evoke qualities lost in the transition to the digital universe.[20]

When contemporary retro-avant-garde photographers such as Fuss or Derges employ historic, often camera-less, 19th-century techniques in a "straight" form, the resulting images are often less visually defined than traditionally printed images, or especially those of digital processing.[21] The work of Adam Fuss (1961–)employs two primary historical techniques, daguerreotypes and camera-less photograms. These result in images that are often not much more than silhouettes. However, the limitations of detail in Fuss's work bring forward other sensual effects in experience, not the least of which is the strong indexical and bodily relationship between image and its source. The bodies so portrayed are not isolated from their environments but imbricated in a field of energy or light, where physical presence and our sensual reception of the image brings out haptic rather than purely optical effects.

In *Love* (1992), Fuss placed two dead rabbits with their entrails on the surface of color photographic paper to make a direct impression of their jewel-like, almost floral character in a photogram silver dye bleach print. A 2015 photogram, *Self Portrait*, created a life-sized image of the artist, floating in a

---

[17] (Sobchack 2004, p. 178).

[18] (Adorno 1997, p. 264).

[19] (Rexer 2002).

[20] Historically, it is certainly the case that there is a small subset of photographers who have always emphasized the ambiguous image. Many of them, such as Oscar Reijlander, Gertrude Käsebier, or Edward Weston, intentionally contradict the more typical ceaseless search for visual acuity with consciously courted arty or abstract effects. The presence of a small number of these exceptional photographers only serves to prove the rule of the photograph's default pursuit of "veracity".

[21] A list of contemporary artists who use analog versions of historic techniques, such as daguerreotypes, photograms, wet-plate collodion, and tintypes would be too extensive to be comprehensively accounted for here, but Sally Mann, Jane Hinds Bidaut, Chuck Close, Luis Gonzales Palma, Takashi Arai, Matthias Olmeta, Floris Neusüss, Vera Lutter, Craig Tuffin, and Kasia Wozniak are just a few representative early-21st century artists creatively employing early-19th-century media. There have been a number of recent surveys of this phenomenon: USC Fisher Gallery, "Lost and Found: Rediscovering Early Photographic Processes" (2001); Rexer's *Photography's Antiquarian Avant-Garde* (2002); The Victoria & Albert Museum, "Shadow Catchers" (2010); and Howard Greenberg Gallery, "A New and Mysterious Art: Ancient Photographic Methods in Contemporary Art" (2016).

pool of water, lit from above, producing a fluid silhouette. Fuss's approach, in which there is often physical contact between the subject and the surface on which the image is made, foregrounds what Alois Riegl would identify as the "haptic". Fuss's long daguerreotype exposures and direct-contact photograms depend on a fusion between a physical presence and the light-sensitive surface on which it makes its presence manifest.[22] In an analysis of similarly grainy and ambiguous imagery in Atom Egoyan's cinema, Jacinto Lageira defines its haptic character as deriving from "a blend of grain and dot patterns of the images ... and also ... from the layers of material which signify in virtue of their depth, the transparency, and so on ... the pictorial treatment of these layers serves a double function in [Atom] Egoyan's films: it serves to reveal or to hide a story; and it veils or unveils an image."[23] The optic mode of consumption imposes an emotional and physical distance from the subject that is destroyed by the haptic's intimate "at-handness". In the haptic character of Fuss's work, and that of other retro-avant-garde photographers, the eye does not scan the image for or become dazed by stupefying details, but it travels across the image as one's hand might traverse it if one's eyes were closed. When Fuss admits that these images carry "much less information" than typical photographs, he notes that the result is "much more intimacy".[24]

In her analysis of "haptic cinema", Laura Marks notes that its images "encourag[e] the viewer to engage with the image through memory", and by working from that interior response, "haptic images can give the impression of seeing for the first time, gradually discovering what is in the image rather than coming to an image already knowing what it is."[25] This quality of feeling as if our sense of sight is new and that images are being formed before our eyes comes about partially because of the material properties and processes of these images. In the mid-1980s, for example, Susan Derges made images of the Chladni effect by vibrating powdered carborundum on photographic paper in order to make a photogram of the resulting patterns. The creation of these images, resulting from a material process, was perceived and felt by the viewer, which reveals formerly invisible material forces. In the 18th century, Ernst Chladni was attempting to find a grammar of music through these physical properties. Adorno suggests that the "all truth of artworks ... iridescently discloses itself in the catastrophic technological progress."[26]

It is the context of the waning of traditional, indexical print photography that the work of Alison Rossiter (1953–) becomes most interesting. Her work is an exploration of the very ground on which photography's historical trajectory is written—the variants of classic photographic paper on which images have been printed. Attending to the ground on which a medium exists and the chemicals which bring images into being, Rossiter's work asserts something like the body of photography itself, the very material reality on which photography's transformative reality depends. After hunting down the remaining stock of now-unavailable classic photographic papers, Rossiter takes the developer and pours and controls its flow over the unexposed, but flawed, surfaces of these hallmark grounds. Her *Eastman Kodak, Velvet Velux, Expiration date December 1926,* (2014) is an example of how her images arise out of the imperfections and gradual degradation of these archaic papers. Its chance effects are a sign of the paper's life in storage and of the passing of time. Rossiter's work reveals this time-lapse effect in a manner reminiscent of Man Ray's *Dust Breeding* (1920/1967) photograph, which chronicled Marcel Duchamp's "work" on the *Large Glass* (1915–23). Duchamp's acceptance of the accumulation of dust on the surface of the work, fixing it into the final configuration of the piece, indicated the passage of time like the sand flowing in an hour glass. Non-intervention, the passive acceptance of the changing conditions without dictatorial human control, the embrace of chance, and even the

---

[22] Alois Riegl first introduces the oppositional pair of haptic and optic in his *Late Roman Art Industry* of 1901; trans. Rolf Winkes Giorgio Bretschneider, 1985.
[23] (Lageira 1996, p. 44).
[24] (Fuss 2010, n.p.).
[25] (Marks 2008, pp. 403–4).
[26] (Adorno [1934] 1990, p. 61).

agency/life of material things are all operational in Rossiter's historical archeology.[27] It is not so much her use of chance effects as her excavation of the image's material origin that relates to *mistical* artistic concerns. This is expressed in the uniquely ambiguous visual character of Rossiter's images, forms one might call, following Chladni, "ur-images"—of the very birth of an image in material form and in sensual apprehension.

6. Conclusions

Our digital datascape is, on the one hand, simply an evolution of the modernist impulse to track and plot the physical world. However, because it does so through bits of information, unmooring its connection to the physical world in order to distribute images across technologies, it has the potential to become a denial of material reality. The artists under discussion here, though, foreground the material processes, presence, and origin of their aesthetic objects. By denying our desire for visual supremacy, they force a sensory adjustment and attunement using other bodily functions and associations. For Sobchack, the danger of electronic cinematic imagery is that it turns its back on the ethical ground of material reality. That ethical, material ground is still available for her in historical [print] photography and in the "subjective animation" of film-based cinema.[28] It is the loosening of the image from its groundedness in the body, its unmooring from any anchoring referentiality, its free-floating signification that loosens its grip on our sensual presence in the world and thus also severs it from history. This homeless form of representation has the most profound implications for the shift from analogue to digital. The gradual independence of the image from its referent is a process that Adorno and Benjamin trace back to the invention of print photography. Noting how print photography "drove out of photographs the shy relation to the speechless subject that still reigned in daguerreotypes", these Frankfurt School philosophers gave an account of what was lost when adopting the new image-technology. Print photography thus replaced the intimacy of the long-exposure daguerreotypes with what Adorno called "photographic sovereignty".[29] There is perhaps no better historical label to extend to new use in our present datascape than "photographic sovereignty". Our present life consists of swimming in a tepid bath of free-floating data-driven imagery, where Virilio's state of substitution reigns.

We are so enamored with our hyper-detailed field of digitized information-laden images that the works of these *mistical* artists may seem like so many ghosts in the machine. Our datascape has enacted a new form of visual orthodoxy. The fact that many of these works, especially the installations of Eliasson and architecture of Diller + Scofidio, but even the unique photographic prints of Fuss, Rossiter and Derges, do not reproduce well across our realm of "ubiquitous photographic" transmission should be embraced as a strength. These *mistical* artists and architects seem rather to demand Renee van de Wall's "tasten denken" (a groping form of thinking through the senses), a close phenomenological parallel to Merleau-Ponty's "palper du regard". In light of the contemporary demands placed on us for data-consumption and distribution, the *mistical* works discussed here offer a recovery of "uncertainty

---

[27] Another fascinating exploration of historical forms of photography, although one that implements very recent digital technology to do so, is Thomas Ruff's photogram series and his imagery based on pornographic images (Nudes, ca. 2003–). In his *Negative* series (2014–), he scans 19th-century vernacular albumen prints, inverts the tonal values, and produces positive C-prints images of the inverted "negative" values in tones of blue. In Ruff's *Photogram* series (2013–), he sets up a virtual darkroom inside computer software, where simulated three-dimensional objects are exposed to light, moved, and manipulated to produce geometric and abstract virtual photograms. In all three of these series, his embrace of the *mistical* and obscure images that result is undertaken with a critical eye to the political implications embedded in this heritage. His is therefore a more conceptual approach than found in the other artists and architects discussed here. See Geoff Dyer, "Porn and the Shadow of Paradise: Thomas Ruff's Nudes," (Dyer 2012) for a summary of the *Nudes* series and Harry Thorne, "Thomas Ruff: Nature Morte," (Thorne 2015) for a discussion of his *Negative* series.

[28] (Sobchack 2004, p. 154). She goes on the claim that electronic imagery creates, "space [that] becomes correlatively experienced as abstract, ungrounded, and flat—a site (or screen) for play and display rather than an invested situation in which action counts rather than computes" (p. 158).

[29] (Adorno [1934/28] 1990, p. 48).

Religions **2019**, *10*, 186

and doubt" of the contingency of bodily knowledge, and of "slow, hesitant and uncertain" "palpating vision".[30]

The slickly produced spectacles that feed our visual appetites provide us with a fleeting fantasy of optical omnipotence and control. In a datascape set on visually recording and plotting everything, works that remain mysterious and ambiguous are far too rare and provide fleeting experiences for "disenchanted moderns who have grown disenchanted with modern disenchantment", in the words of Kosky.[31] Rather than viewing and experiencing misty, foggy, and ambiguous forms and spaces as lacking information, where "blur is understood as loss", we can instead embrace Elizabeth Diller's notion that blur "can also be thought positively".[32] The shadows, shrouds, and films of obfuscating mists found in these works elicit a bodily response to their materiality, one that foregrounds our continuity with space, our belongingness to it. It is a *mistical* version of Jane Bennet's "vibrant matter". If modernist philosophy is dependent on reifying the distinction between subject and object, of clarifying the particularities of difference, the vital materialist instead lingers at the recognition of mutuality of subject and object, at those moments "during which they find themselves fascinated by objects [and space], taking them as clues to the material vitality that they share with them."[33]

Funding: This research was partially supported through the Roger Williams University Foundation to Promote Scholarship and Teaching.

Conflicts of Interest: The author declares no conflict of interest.

References

Adorno, Theodor W. ; Translated by Thomas Y. Levin. 1990. The Curves of the Needle. *October* 55: 48–55. First published 1927/28. [CrossRef]

Adorno, Theodor W. ; Translated by Thomas Y. Levin. 1990. The Form of the Phonograph Record. *October* 55: 56–61. First published 1934. [CrossRef]

Adorno, Theodor W. 1997. *Aesthetic Theory*. Translated and Edited by Robert Hullot-Kentor. Minneapolis: The University of Minnesota Press.

Benjamin, Walter. 1992. The Work of Art in the Age of Mechanical Reproduction. In *Art in Modern Culture: An Anthology of Critical Texts*. Edited by Francis Frascina and Jonathan Harris. London: Phaidon Press Limited, pp. 297–307. First published 1936.

Bennet, Jane. 2010. *Vibrant Matter: A Political Ecology of Things*. Durham: Duke University Press.

Choi, Jung. 2014. Conceptual Laboratory of Depth: Olafur Eliasson's Your Atmospheric Colour Atlas. *Sztuka i Dokumentacja* 10: 61–66.

Diller, Elizabeth. 2002. Blur/Babble. In *Blur: The Making of Nothing*. New York: Harry Abrams, Originally published as 2001. *Anything*. Edited by Cynthia Davidson. Cambridge: MIT Press.

Dyer, Geoff. 2012. Porn and the Shadow of Paradise: Thomas Ruff's Nudes. *The Guardian*. March 2. Available online: https://www.theguardian.com/artanddesign/2012/mar/02/porn-shadow-side-paradise-thomas-ruff (accessed on 8 November 2017).

Fuss, Adam. 2010. Video Interview for the Victoria and Albert Museum's Shadow Catchers. Available online: https://vimeo.com/13149236 (accessed on 1 November 2017).

Kosky, Jeffrey L. 2013. *Arts of Wonder: Enchanting Secularity—Walter DeMaria, Diller + Scofidio, James Turrell, Andy Goldsworthy*. Chicago: University of Chicago Press.

Lageira, Jacinto. 1996. Scenario of the Untouchable Body. *Public* 13: 32–47.

Marks, Laura U. 2000. *The Skin of the Film: Intercultural Cinema, Embodiment, and the Senses*. Durham: Duke University Press.

---

[30] (van de Wall 2008, p. 5). Van de Wall herself makes explicit the connection between her *tasten denken* and Merleau-Ponty's phenomenology (5).
[31] (Kosky 2013, p. 176).
[32] (Diller [2001] 2002, p. 133).
[33] (Bennet 2010, p. 16).

Marks, Laura U. 2008. Haptic Cinema. In *Visual Sense: A Cultural Reader*. Edited by Elizabeth Edwards and Kaushik Bhaumik. Brooklyn: Berg Pub., pp. 399–407.

Paterson, Mark. 2016. Architecture of Sensation: Affect, Motility and the Oculomotor. *Body & Society* 23: 3–35.

Rexer, Lyle. 2002. *Photography's Antiquarian Avant-Garde: The New Wave in Old Processes*. New York: Harry N. Abrams.

Sobchack, Vivian. 2004. *Carnal Thoughts: Embodiment and Moving Image Culture*. Berkeley: University of California Press.

Elizabeth, Ströker. 1965. *Investigations in Philosophy of Space*. Translated by Algis Mickunas. Athens: Ohio University Press.

Thompson, Nato, ed. 2012. *Living as Form: Socially Engaged Art from 1991–2011*. New York: Creative Book.

Thorne, Harry. 2015. Thomas Ruff: Nature Morte. *Studio International*. originally published 27 August 2015. Available online: http://www.studiointernational.com/index.php/thomas-ruff-nature-morte-reiew-gagosian-gallery-london-photography-negatives (accessed on 2 December 2017).

van de Wall, Renee. 2008. *At the Edges of Vision*. Farnham: Ashgate Publishing.

Virilio, Paul. 2000. *The Information Bomb*. Translated by Chris Turner. London: Verso. First published 1998.

Wilson, Luoise, and Paul Virilio. 1994. Interview with Paul Virilio. Cyberwar, God and Television: Interview with Paul Virilio. *CTheory.org*. Available online: http://www.ctheory.net/articles.aspx?id=62 (accessed on 1 December 2018).

Article

Beyond Belief: Chance, Authorship, and the Limits of Comprehension in Gerhard Richter's *Strip*

James Romaine

Art Department, Lander University, Greenwood, SC 29649, USA; jromaine@lander.edu

Received: 2 February 2019; Accepted: 12 April 2019; Published: 17 April 2019

Abstract: For nearly six decades, Gerhard Richter has challenged the conceptual and visual limits of contemporary painting. His 2011 work *Strip* overloads the viewer's visual perception. Richter created this unique digital print using a process that deliberately employs chance to circumvent the artist's authorship. This article examines the history of Richter's skepticism of creative authority and the strategies he has developed to realize an art that exceeds the limits of human skill and imagination. Although he remains an atheist, Richter frames his pursuit of an incomprehensible art in terms of a longing for a belief in God.

Keywords: Gerhard Richter; contemporary painting; *Strip*; chance; belief; skepticism; authorship; abstract painting; Cologne Cathedral window

---

Strip (921-6) is a unique digital print by Gerhard Richter.[1] This sensational 2011 work, in the permanent collection of the Tate Modern, London, is arguably one of the most conceptually fresh and art historically important works by the contemporary German artist. In both its visual presence and the process of its creation, *Strip* evidences an organic life that exceeds the limits of the artist's authorship and the viewer's perception. It is a model of a reality in which creativity and chance realize an other-worldly beauty that is the materialization of what Richter called, "the highest form of hope."[2]

According to Richter, our capacity to believe in the existence of something greater than ourselves, something that is incomprehensible to the human mind, is our greatest human characteristic. He further asserts that art is the only means of realizing that belief in material and present form. In notes to himself, dated 3 January 1988 and published in his collected writings, interviews, and letters, Richter wrote, "Art is a pure realization of religious feeling, capacity for faith, longing for God." But then he continues, following this confident pronouncement with a caution,

> All other realizations of these [religious feeling, capacity for faith, longing for God], the outstanding human qualities, abuse these qualities by exploiting them: that is by serving an ideology. Even art becomes 'applied art' just as soon as it gives up freedom from function and set out to convey a message. Art is human only in the absolute refusal to make a statement.

However, Righter concludes this written thought to himself on a more optimistic note, "The ability to believe is our outstanding quality, and only art adequately translates it into reality. But when we assuage our need for faith with ideology, we court disaster."[3]

---

1   Between 2010 and 2015, Richter created eighty-six digital prints, all of these are entitled *Strip*. The designation *(921-6)* is from Richter's self-created Catalogue Raisonné and serves to distinguish this work from the rest of the series. This Catalogue Raisonné is part of the artist's website, gerhard-richter.com. Hereafter, the title *Strip* will only be used in reference to *Strip (921-6)*.

2   "Text for catalog of *documenta* 7, Kassel, 1982" in (Richter et al. 2009, p. 121).

3   "Notes, 1988" in (Richter et al. 2009, p. 200).

Richter has had, from the very beginning of his career, a belief in painting and a suspicion of artistic authorship. This contradiction has motivated him to push the conceptual and technical limits of painting for nearly six decades. From his paintings based on banal media and family photos to his mastery of a technique of smearing abstract skins of paint with a squeegee tool that he developed himself, Richter has been one of the most conceptually astute and technically facile painters of the past half century. While much of the abstract painting produced in this period has been either, on the one hand, heir to the modernist conception of the work of art as the expression of the artist's inner feeling or, on the other hand, cynical end-game musings on the theoretical "death of painting," Richter's methodical pursuit of a third path consistently has been conceptually innovative and visually spellbinding.[4]

Richter has been richly rewarded for his efforts. He is one of the most commercially successful and critically acclaimed living artists.[5] He is regularly counted, by art critics and curators, among the most important living painters. The voluminous literature on his art, from scholarly articles, to exhibition catalogs, to monographs, evidences how Richter is one of the widely celebrated and sharply contested contemporary artists.

Every work of art proposes a way of looking at the world. It makes this proposition not only in *what* it depicts but also in *how* it depicts. *Strip* challenges the viewer's senses; it overloads the viewer's visual perception. If the senses are how the viewer apprehends the world, Richter presents the viewer with the limitations and potential impairments of these tools. This essay examines *Strip* as a fulfillment of Richter's pursuit of an art that is, paradoxically, a realization of our capacity to believe without falling into what he regards as the fallacy of personal expression. Rather than speaking to the viewer about politics or religion, Richter's art confronts the self-aware viewer with both the limitations of their own present-state being and the prospect of a reality that is beyond our comprehension.[6]

1. Encountering the Incomprehensible

Measuring 200 × 440 cm, *Strip* is composed of countless thin horizontal bands of different colors. These lines are perfectly straight, parallel, and run from one edge of the work to the other. Their optical velocity is unconstrained by any frame within or around *Strip*.[7]

Strip is majestic and hallucinatory. Its lateral rush of color has no discernable composition or focal point. The pulsating strokes of nonmimetic color do not repeat in any vertical pattern. And yet, Richter's work is visually balanced and harmonious. This work is slightly more than twice as long as it is high. This gives the work a visual impression of material growth. Unified by a limited range of color (both hue and value), *Strip* has an indefinable, but certainly recognizable, organic beauty.

Strip exceeds the possibilities of traditional painting or drawing. Reproducing this digital print by hand, to draw countless perfectly straight lines that measured 440 cm in length, would be nearly impossible. As such, the work immediately announces itself as a digital creation.

While these perfectly straight and parallel threads of color seem to run from one edge of the work to the other without interruption, *Strip*, in fact, has a midpoint divide. This seam is not perceptible in reproduction but Richter's online Catalogue Raisonné identifies that this work has "2 parts."

---

[4] Painters, working in abstraction, whose work might be considered, at least by them, an expression of their inner expression include Ross Bleckner, Yayoi Kusama, the artist collective Tim Rollins and K.O.S., and *Julian Schnabel*. Painters whose work could be described as embracing the so-called "death of painting," include Daniel Buren, Peter Halley, and Allan McCollum.

[5] Richter's achievements in the art market, the countless exhibitions of his art around the world, and the voluminous literature on his work are all meticulously documented on his website, gerhard-richter.com.

[6] After employing a careful examination of *Strip*, and its process of creation, to frame the question of creative authorship in Richter's art, this essay traces the personal and artistic maturation that brought Richter to the *Strip Paintings*. The essay concludes with an examination of the issue of chance and authorship that Richter's oeuvre raises as well as his proposition that painting can address, if not fully satisfy, the fundamental human longing for God.

[7] Some other prints from the *Strip Painting* series do have borders.

This vertical seam in *Strip* is not actually *necessary* to the work. There are prints from the *Strip Painting* series, measuring more than twice as long as the work at the Tate Modern, that are one single piece.[8] However, this vertical break in the horizontal midpoint is intentional and conceptually essential to the work. *Strip* is a unique work; as such it participates in a conversation about "aura" in contemporary art. But, at the same time, *Strip* is composed of two identical parts.[9] These twin halves of *Strip* are each 200 × 220 cm. They are nearly square, which gives them a visual solidity. Each partner maintains its individuality within the totality of the work. However, since the right half is a perfect reproduction of the left and the left is a perfect reproduction of the right, *Strip* exemplifies the aura and its double.

Strip has a powerful visual presence. As part of Gerhard Richter's continuous investigation of painting within the photographic and digital age, *Strip* is one of the most visually engaging and conceptually clever works within an already impressive oeuvre.

There is no way to completely see *Strip*. It is taller than many viewers and, since it doesn't rest on the floor, about half of these bands of color are higher than the average viewer. If one stands back from the work, far enough for the work to remain within the viewer's field of vision, the lines are too small to be visually differentiated. They begin to optically blur, but this creates new lines. In fact, as one approaches *Strip*, starting from across the gallery, the discernable bands of color seem to spontaneously multiply with each step. One line becomes two, four, eight new lines. One color becomes two, four, eight new colors. The closer that we get to the work, the more colors and lines magically appear. There is a sense that if we could somehow get even closer, that there could be more bands within bands of color than we haven't yet perceived.

Could one actually count the lines in *Strip*? Possibly. But they exceed what the eye and mind of the viewer standing in the gallery can comprehend. Without actually being infinite, these striations evoke infinity. There is a palpable impression that there is an unfathomable world within *Strip* that we might be able to step into.

Strip's expansive length and its nearly hallucinogenic vibration of color creates a perception, particularly if one is standing near the center and close to the work, that it extends endlessly. Even when we are visually able to find the edges, *Strip* evokes a reality that has no beginning or end or edges. Through *Strip*, we transgress into the realm of the unknowable.

While *Strip* provides the viewer with visual enchantment, it also poses a challenge to anyone tasked with finding words to describe this experience. As Richter himself noted, "To talk about painting is not only difficult but perhaps pointless, too. You can only express in words what words are capable of expressing, what language can communicate. Painting has nothing to do with that."[10] And yet, Richter is one of the most verbally articulate and insightful contemporary visual artists. The published collection of his writings and interviews, from 1961 to 2007, runs more than 500 pages. As much as any living artist, the literature on Richter's art is constructed around his own characterization of his art.

One term that Richter repeatedly employs in discussing his art is "incomprehensible."[11] In notes to himself, dated 1981, Richter described his aim being, "Painting is the making of an analogy for

---

8   Strip 930-1, 930-2, 930-4, and 930-6 are each 1000 cm long. Strip 930-7 measures 1100 cm in length. All of these are one piece.

9   Within the *Strip Paintings* series, there are also works that are divided into three and four identical units. The vertical divides in these *Strip* works also make reference to one of Richter's most admired artists, the Abstract Expressionist painter Barnett Newman. Also, the division of these works into identical units, places Richter's art in the company of Minimalist and Post-minimalist painting. However, the contribution of *Strip* to the history of abstract painting is outside the scope of this essay.

10   Gerhard Richter in (Belz 2012).

11   The concept of "incomprehensibility" has numerous histories and interpretations within various philosophical and religious traditions. However, the question that concerns this essay is "what does 'the incomprehensible' mean to Richter and how is this, then, manifested in his methods and works of art?" Rather than diverging into tangents of what "incomprehensibility" might mean within sundry philosophical and religious traditions (which Richter may or may not have studied and which he, in all likelihood, would have rejected) this essay focusses on a close examination of Richter's extensive writings and interviews to formulate a better understanding of the artist's evolving beliefs.

something non-visual and *incomprehensible*: giving it form and bringing it within reach. And that is why good paintings are *incomprehensible*."[12] Richter returned to this idea in notes from 1985, stating that, to his achieve his aim, his process should be "painting like nature, painting as change, becoming, emerging, being-there, ... and *incomprehensible*."[13] These are incomprehensible means to realize incomprehensible ends. And, in a 1998 interview, Richter told Mark Rosenthal, "the structure of my works is so complicated and difficult so that they are *incomprehensible* .... If you want, you may call it metaphysical."[14]

Richter has also used "incomprehensible" to describe God. In a 2011 interview, he described the complex contradictions of his doubts and beliefs saying, "we can't exist without some form of belief in things .... Even as an atheist, I believe. We are just built that way." He added, "I believe that you always have to believe ... But I can't believe in God, as such, he's either too big or too small for me, and always *incomprehensible*, unbelievable."[15] In that same interview, Richter said that a successful painting must have "something *incomprehensible*, something that is on a higher plane."[16]

These 1998 and 2011 interviews bracket the genesis of Richter's *Strip Paintings* series, and suggest the direction of Richter's thinking that brought him to *Strip*. While he aspires for his art to have metaphysical content, Richter achieves this spiritual aim through material and rational means, by extending material and logic beyond itself. If the incomprehensibility of any structure in a work of art is its measure of metaphysical effect, *Strip* is absolutely metaphysical.

2. Creating *Strip*

To create *Strip*, Richter started with a photograph of one his own paintings, *Abstract Painting (724-4)*.[17] This 1990 painting is visually rich in color and detail, making it ideal for Richter's process. He began by scanning a photograph of *Abstract Painting*. Starting with a detail of this scanned image, he then used a computer to systematically rework the image by first vertically dividing it and then joining each of the halves with a mirror image of itself. This created two new images, and two new starting points. Richter, using a computer, repeated this process twelve times. One picture was multiplied into two; two became four; four became eight. Richter continued this process until he had four thousand and ninety-six unique images. By this point, the image of *Abstract Painting* had been transformed into eight thousand one hundred and ninety striations of color that were, each, only 0.00762 cm wide.

Richter selected, discarded, and recombined these narrow strips. It was previously noted that each example from the *Strip Painting* series is unified by a limited range of color. This is evidence of Richter's creative intervention into and reorganization of the eight thousand one hundred and ninety strips created by the computer. He then used a process of mirroring to extend these strips into the horizontal bands of color that stretch across the work we encounter at the Tate Modern.

The process of creating *Strip* is simultaneously logical and random, methodical and intuitive. Richter documented this process of artist-directed chance in a book *Gerhard Richter: Patterns: Divided, Mirrored, Repeated*.[18] Looking through the book, it is possible, at first, to follow the process. While it requires concentration, it is manageable to track how the detail of one page becomes multiplied on the next *several* pages (since at each stage the number of new images is compounded). *Abstract Painting*

---

12 "Notes, 1981" in (Richter et al. 2009, p. 120). Italics added.
13 "Notes, 1985" in (Richter et al. 2009, p. 142). Italics added.
14 "Interview with Mark Rosenthal, 1998" in (Richter et al. 2009, p. 330). Italics added.
15 "I Have Nothing to Say and I'm Saying It." in (Godfrey et al. 2016, p. 24). Italics added.
16 "I Have Nothing to Say and I'm Saying It." in (Godfrey et al. 2016, p. 22). Italics added.
17 All the prints from the *Strip Painting* series are derived from *Abstract Painting (724-4)*. Like *Strip (921-6)*, *Abstract Painting (724-4)* can be distinguished from Richter's other paintings, also titled *Abstract Painting*, by its Catalogue Raisonné number. Hereafter, the title *Abstract Painting* will only be used in reference to *Abstract Painting (724-4)*. *Abstract Painting* is in a private collection, it sold at Christie's in 2006 for $1,338,434.
18 (Richter 2012)

becomes a set of increasingly intricate patterns. It is fun, at first, to even try to look at a page and try to imagine (by dividing, mirroring, and repeating in the mind) how the next page/pages might look.

However, as eight becomes sixteen and sixteen become thirty-two, one begins to lose track of the process. By sixty-four, the viewer is likely to become increasingly lost in the process and, by one hundred and twenty-eight, it became useless to even try to follow the evolution and multiplication of the images. Richter must have recognized this breaking point himself because, after sixty-four, the book only reproduces select examples from the last six stages of transformation. (To reproduce every image from every stage would require a book of eight thousand one hundred and ninety pages.) However, *Gerhard Richter: Patterns: Divided, Mirrored, Repeated* is instructive. It allows the reader to trace a process that is at first logical and finally becomes incomprehensible. It allows the reader to find the breaking point of their concentration, of the limits of their imagination.

3. The Problem of Painting

Strip is part of a series that Richter began in 2010. Despite the fact that these works are unique inkjet prints, this series is collectively titled *Strip Paintings* and *Strip* is listed in Richter's Catalogue Raisonné as a painting.[19] By designating these digitally created abstract images as "paintings," Richter provocatively challenges the definition of "painting" in a digital age.[20] But there is, potentially, something even more significant at stake in calling *Strip* a painting. If we consider a "painting" to be a unique and handmade work of art and a "print" to be mechanically created multiple, "painting" has an inherent authoritative voice. Richter acknowledges this when he said, "I like how Adorno explained it: you can't put pictures together. Paintings are always 'mortal enemies' . . . . Every painting is an assertion that tolerates no company."[21] Every painting asserts its position as an authoritative statement about how to see the world. Situating *Strip*, which is a mechanically created unique work, in the category of "painting" enables Richter to address what might be the central issue of his artistic project, namely the problem of an authoritative voice that painting might suppose.

Strip, and its related works from the *Strip Painting* series, represents one of the most significant developments in Richter's entire oeuvre. However, this essay is not primarily concerned with what the *Strip Painting* series might mean for painting in a digital age, which is a question mainly of interest for art theorists, or whether these unique digital works should be counted as paintings at all, which is a question mainly of concern for the art market.[22] This essay explores *Strip* and the *Strip Painting* series as a culmination of Richter's artistic method and his skeptical attitude toward artistic authorship. By situating Richter's *Strip* within his oeuvre, we can examine it as the fulfillment of a career-long maturation process in the purpose and visual strategies of his art. Therefore, before exploring the issues of chance and authorship evidenced in *Strip*, we should briefly trace some of the personal and artistic evolution that brought Richter to this work.

---

[19] The *Strip Painting* series are cataloged in Richter's own Catalogue Raisonné as "paintings," even though he has a section for "prints." Works from the *Strip Painting* series have been exhibited in several gallery shows, including *Gerhard Richter: Painting 2010–2011*, Galerie Marian Goodman, Paris, France, 23 September 2011–3 November 2011 and *Gerhard Richter: Painting 2012*, Marian Goodman Gallery, New York, USA, 12 September 2012–13 October 2012. The point is that Richter has repeatedly asserted that these unique digital prints belong, in his mind, within his painting oeuvre.

[20] There are market reasons why Richter would categorize these large unique prints as "paintings." However, across his career Richter has both shown an indifference to the art market as well as a commitment to continually challenging the boundaries of "painting." Richter has said, "Today I find that art mostly has to fulfill economic conditions. That's no good either. Art had to be truthful—that's its moral aspect" (van Bruggen 1985, p. 82).

[21] Gerhard Richter in (Belz 2012). Presumably, since they are by nature not unique, photographs and prints have no choice but to tolerate the company of other images.

[22] For a discussion of what the *Strip Painting* series might mean for the current state of painting, see (Buchloh 2012).

4. Formative Experiences

The paradoxes of his art, his suspicion of creative authorship and his embrace of artist-directed chance, are, in part, rooted in the complexity of Richter's early life experiences, first under Nazism and then under Soviet Communism, as well as his education at the Dresden Art Academy.

Richter was born February 9th, 1932 in Dresden, Germany. During the years of the Second World War, he lived in the village of Waltersdorf with his mother Hildegard and sister Gisela. His father, Horst, who had been a teacher, was conscripted into the military. Waltersdorf is about 60 *miles* north of Dresden and was spared the type of devastation that Dresden suffered under Allied bombing. Richter was enrolled in the Hitler Youth but found ways of avoiding participation. By his own account, he had little direct experience of the war and has few memories of that period. Nevertheless, this formative experience impressed upon Richter the violence to which total belief in an ideology could, perhaps inevitably, give birth.

In 1951, Richter returned to the ruins of Dresden and began to study at the Dresden Art Academy (Hochschule für Bildende Künste Dresden). Since 1949, Germany had been divided between the Western Allies and the Soviet Union. Dresden was in the German Democratic Republic (GDR), often called East Germany. At the Dresden Art Academy, Richter had a classical visual art education that emphasized drawing and representation. At the academy, Richter was taught that all forms of technique are ideological and that art found its purpose in the service of advancing the messages of the state. For example, at the academy, traditional realism was championed while modernist abstraction was suppressed, for ideological reasons. But the result of this formative training is that Richter is fundamentally suspicious of all technique.

Richter graduated from the Dresden Art Academy in 1956. The academy's principal mission was to prepare artist-workers for state service, such as painting murals for public buildings and designing political posters. Richter did both of these but he was certain that his life and artistic career lay in the West. In 1959, when travel from East Germany to West Germany was still permissible, Richter had visited *Documenta II*.[23] There he saw the work of Jackson Pollock and Lucio Fontana. Richter was particularly impressed by Pollock and saw in his work an authenticity that was absent in the ideologically directed art of East Germany. Speaking of Pollock and Fontana, Richter told Benjamin H.D. Buchloh "I might almost say that those paintings were the real reason why I left the GDR. I realized that there was something wrong with my whole way of thinking."[24] In 1961, Richter and his first wife, Marianne Eufinger, escaped to West Germany.[25]

This period of Richter's life, education, and artistic beginnings is characterized by a personal resistance to the imposition of ideology. It instilled in him a skepticism of creative authorship and authoritative voices. This cultivated a commitment to a process that eschews both ideology and technique. Richter described this practice as "letting a thing come, rather than creating it—no assertions, constructions, formulations, inventions, ideology—in order to gain access to all that is genuine, richer, more alive: to what is beyond my understanding."[26] While his strategies in his art have evolved, his work has been persistently guided by a profound skepticism that can be traced to his youth.

5. God

The aversion to all ideology that Richter's life under the totalizing systems of Nazism and Communism instilled in him also manifested itself in a skepticism of institutional religion and a disbelief in the existence of God. In a 1993 interview, Richter said, "By the age of sixteen or seventeen I

---

[23] *Documenta* II was held 11 July and 1 October 1959, in Kassel, Germany.

[24] "Interview with Benjamin H.D. Buchloh, 1986" in (Richter et al. 2009, p. 163).

[25] Richter has been married three times. He married Marianne Eufinger in 1957; they had a daughter and were divorced in 1982. In the same year, Richter married the sculptor Isa Genzken; they were divorced in 1994. Richter married Sabine Moritz in 1995 and they have three children.

[26] "Notes, 1985" in (Richter et al. 2009, p. 140).

was absolutely clear that there is no God—an alarming discovery to me, after my Christian upbringing. By that time, my fundamental aversion to all beliefs and ideologies was fully developed."[27]

By his "Christian upbringing" Gerhard Richter was referencing his father's faith. Horst Richter was a fervent Protestant. When Richter referred to his "Christian upbringing," he was speaking only of his father. His mother, Hildegard Schönfelder, did not share her husband's devoutness. She regarded her husband as intellectually and culturally inferior.

However, Horst was a poor role model. As a teacher, he was required to join the Nazi party. Then he was drafted into Hitler's military. Horst was captured and spent the rest of the war in an American prisoner-of-war camp. Although Horst had no enthusiasm for politics or war, they defined his life. He returned home unable to resume his role as a teacher, husband, or father. The accumulation of these failures became cause for Mother to ridicule Horst and his piety. As Richter's youth imbued in him a distrust of ideology, authority, and father figures, these doubts coalesced in his doubts about God.

Richter's disbelief in God may have also been related to his suspicion of his own creative authorship (although it is not possible to say which of these is impetus for the other). However, just as his doubts about creative authorship have not kept him from the studio, his doubts about God did not keep him from having his children baptized in the church.

Richter's three youngest children, Moritz (born 1995), Ella Maria (born 1996), and Theodor (born 2006), were all baptized in Cologne Cathedral.[28] Speaking in 2001, Richter said, "I was very moved when our two children were baptized."[29] In 2002, Richter was commissioned to create a window for the south transept of Cologne Cathedral.

The fact that Richter elected to have his three youngest children baptized in a religious ceremony as well as his acceptance of a commission for such a high-profile overtly religious work of art are signs of a potential evolution in Richter's stance towards Christianity, and Catholicism in particular.

As a teenager, Richter had confidently concluded that God did not exist. However, in 1998, Richter told an interviewer that, as he was getting older (he was then sixty-six), he was also changing his views on faith. "I am less antagonistic to 'the holy', to the spiritual experience, these days. It is part of us, and we need that quality."[30]

In a 2004 interview, Richter said, "I sympathize with the Catholic Church. I can't believe in God, but I think the Catholic Church is marvelous." And he added, "When we had our two children christened here in the cathedral, my attitude towards the church had already radically changed, and I had slowly begun to realize what the church can offer, how much meaning it can convey, how much help, comfort and security."[31]

While the list of 20th century and contemporary visual artists who regard their art as having a spiritual dimension but have eschewed institutional religion is too long to count, Richter is a perhaps unusual case of an artist who embraces institutional religion while remaining skeptical of spirituality.

6. Cathedral Window

In 2002, Richter was commissioned to create a window for the south transept of Cologne Cathedral.[32] Completed three years before Richter began his *Strip Painting* series, *Cathedral Window* is an important precedent for the process of design, chance, repetition, and mirroring that Richter employed in *Strip*.

---

27 "Interview with Hans Ulrich Obrist, 1993" in (Richter et al. 2009, p. 288).

28 Moritz, Ella Maria, and Theodor were all born to Richter's third wife Sabine Moritz (married in 1995). Richter also has a daughter Babette, also known as Betty, (born 1966) with his first wife Marianne 'Ema' Eufinge. Richter has lived in Cologne since 1983.

29 (Storr 2003, p. 141).

30 "Interview with Mark Rosenthal" in (Richter et al. 2009, p. 331).

31 "Interview with Jan Thorn-Prikker, 2004" in (Richter et al. 2009, p. 471).

32 For a more extensive discussion of the commission, a contextualizing of this work's visual, conceptual, and spiritual aspects within Richter's oeuvre, and the window's contested reception, see (Romaine 2009).

The original cathedral window had been destroyed in WWII. The opportunity to create work for such a historically significant building and such a publicly prominent site represented an important milestone in the recognition of Richter as one of Germany's leading artists. Furthermore, since, at that time two of his children had been baptized in this cathedral, the commission was also personally significant for Richter.

The commission specified that the window depict six Christian martyrs of the 20th century. While he accepted the commission, Richter found himself unable to fulfill the expected figurative motifs. Then, the solution presented itself, by coincidence. Richter recalled,

> Of course I was impressed by this honorable request, but I soon realized that I was absolutely not up to the task. After a few failed attempts to approach the theme, and when I was almost at the point of giving up entirely, an illustration of *4096 Colors* landed on the table. I placed the template of the window's frame on it and saw that this was the only possibility.[33]

Richter found the solution for *Cathedral Window*, by chance, in a work from 1974, *4096 Colors*.[34] Richter described the process of creating *4096 Colors* saying, "the hope is that this way a painting will emerge that is more than I could invent."[35]

For *Cathedral Window*, Richter worked with 72 colors. He used a computer to generate patterns. He then selected some of these chance-created configurations and rejected others. To give the window a sense of symmetry, he mirrored the composition. This is clearly evident in the lancet windows. For example, in the three lancet windows at the left, a design that is based on the randomly allotted sequence of squares begins at the left and proceeds to the center. But the right half of these three lancet windows is a mirror of the first half.

In a sermon delivered in a special installation Mass, on 25 August 2007, cathedral prelate Josef Sauerborn pronounced, "In chance, the unexpected and unforeseen is hidden. Chance becomes a cipher for the mysterious that transcends our mental capacity." Sauerborn added, "God is not computable; he cannot be contained in any system."[36]

The window gives color and light a material presence. In notes dated 1964–1965, Richter wrote, "The central problem in my painting is light"[37] While his window for Cologne Cathedral is a fulfillment of that ambition, this strategy is also evidenced in *Strip*.

7. Abstract Painting

If *Cathedral Window* is one precedent for the process of artist-guided chance that generated *Strip*, the visual origin of this unique digital print can be found in *Abstract Painting (724-4)*. Painted in 1990, *Abstract Painting* is a large (92 × 126 cm) and vibrant work.

To create *Abstract Painting*, Richter employed a tool that he invented himself. In the Richter literature, this tool is most often called a "squeegee." However, if this term evokes the idea of a strip of rubber attached to a stick, that is not at all what Richter uses. These squeegees, of various sizes, are custom-made tools of bendable, but firm, sheets of Perspex with an attached wood handle that runs the full length of squeegee.

Richter employs these squeegees like large palette knives. He is able to pull, scrape, and smear the surface of his painting. The Perspex blade leaves behind a commensurate paint surface, except that there are places where the surface has been torn open to reveal the layers below. The result of the method creates a surface that retains a freshness, as if, even years later, the surface still reads as wet.

---

[33] (Elger 2009, p. 352).
[34] Catalogue Raisonné: 359
[35] "Notes, 1985" in (Richter et al. 2009, p. 140).
[36] (Romaine 2009, p. 52).
[37] "Notes, 1964–1965" in (Richter et al. 2009, p. 35).

Painters such as Gustave Courbet and J.M.W. Turner, for example, had used the palette knife to smear the paint surface. This method allowed them to highlight the materiality of their paint as surface. However, the small size of the traditional palette knife still left a trace of the artist's hand. Courbet and Turner were exchanging one type of mark, the brushstroke, for a different type of mark made with the knife. Richter uses squeegees that are large enough to cover the entire painting's surface in a single stroke. This eliminates the appearance of the artist's hand.

Richter's squeegee method creates a surface that reads as mechanical rather than handmade. In a 1985 interview with Dorothea Dietrich, Richter acknowledged that these squeegee-created abstractions, despite having a flat, impersonal, surface, still evidence his touch. Richter noted, "I want to avoid at all costs that this personal expression be too direct."[38] Speaking of gestural abstraction, Richter added, "Everybody does it and it is very easy. This type of authenticity can be found in many paintings, but in the long run it becomes rather boring."[39] He then contrasted gestural abstraction with his own method of artist-guided chance saying, "I like to compare my process of making art to the composition of music. There, all personal expression has been subjugated to the structure ... "[40]

The mechanical feel of these abstractions has been consistently interpreted in the Richter literature as his commentary on the state of painting in an age of mechanical, and then digital, reproduction. But Richter's works are more than philosophical musings on the state of painting. Works such as *Abstract Painting* employ a use of chance, guided by a combination of creative intuition (mind), exacting attention to detail (eye), and precise technical expertise (hand) that Richter has developed over a lifetime in the studio, to present the viewer with a model of looking at, thinking about, and acting in the world. Reading Richter's paintings—visually navigating their surfaces and conceptually excavating their processes of formation—challenges the viewer to see and think in certain directions. They equip us as the viewer to be more critically self-aware of our own precarious state. And yet the unadulterated beauty of *Strip* and *Abstract Painting* suggests that all is not lost. We need not abandon hope. The very existence of these works of art offers proof of potential, belief that the inconceivable is possible.

Richter does not regard these so-called "abstract" paintings as nonrepresentational. He said, "Almost all the abstract paintings show scenarios, surroundings or landscapes that don't exist, but they create the impression that they could exist. As though they were photographs of scenarios and regions that had never been seen, that could never exist."[41]

Richter's paintings, such as *Strip* and *Abstract Painting*, are not abstractions of a representational, i.e., visible or perceptible, world. One can think of *Strip* and *Abstract Painting* as exactingly detailed representations (like a painting by Jan van Eyck) of a world that is imperceptible. As representations of "scenarios and regions that had never been seen," it is important to note that *Strip* and *Abstract Painting* are entirely nonpictorial. *Abstract Painting* has material depth, layers created by the squeegee pulling layers of paint over each other, with the underlayers being revealed in the tears of the surface. However, this depth is the result of the painting's material structure, not an illusion of pictorial depth. In pictorial abstraction, such as the works of Kandinsky, the image is nonrepresentational but still retains the characteristics of a pictorial illusion. This method of pictorial illusion, such as it was developed in the Renaissance, was designed to facilitate images, illusions, in which the world depicted more closely corresponded to the world of the viewer. Richter's use of the squeegee entirely eliminates the pictorial. As such, the "scenarios and regions" to which they gain the viewer access is a world that is made materially present by the painting but that is also somehow completely unlike the world of the viewer.

If Richter believes that works such as *Abstract Painting* are representations of an incomprehensible reality, the *Strip Paintings* series is, in part, a test of that proposition. The process of creating *Strip* from *Abstract Painting* is a journey into the "regions that had never been seen." For Richter, this is a discovery

---

[38] "Interview with Dorothea Dietrich, 1985" in (Richter et al. 2009, p. 145).
[39] "Interview with Dorothea Dietrich, 1985" in (Richter et al. 2009, p. 145).
[40] "Interview with Dorothea Dietrich, 1985" in (Richter et al. 2009, p. 145).
[41] "I Have Nothing to Say and I'm Saying It." in (Godfrey et al. 2016, p. 19).

of worlds within worlds. From one work, Richter could produce, potentially, an infinite number of unique prints. In each print, the strip could be infinitely mirrored to stretch it to any length. *Strip* is a world beyond representation.

8. Gaining Access to the Unvisualizable

The squeegee-created abstract painting represented the most significant development in Richter's art since the beginning of his mature work in 1962. These works differ in both process and concept from his early abstractions. He noted, "What's new about these abstract paintings is the fact that they were not copied from a photograph, nor were they traced from a side-projection of a sketch. Rather, they were freely composed on the canvas."[42]

Being "freely composed on the canvas," the squeegee abstractions introduced the element of chance into his painting process. Previously, Richter had attempted to curtail his authorship through the use of photography. However, these photo-based paintings still evidenced his artistic touch. Richter's blurring of his images had become a sort of signature.

Since the painting created with the squeegee cannot be predicted, Richter relinquishes some control over the painting. But, with practice, the squeegee can be guided. Through the angle of the tool, the pressure applied, as well as the direction and duration of action, he can intervene into the process, as he put it, "giving form to chance, putting it to use."[43] However, the visual compositions and colors left behind by the squeegee are unplanned as are the rips in the painting's material surface, which allows previously buried layers of paint to become unexpectedly visible.

Richter noted, to himself, "When I paint an abstract picture (the problem is very much the same in other cases), I neither know in advance what it is meant to look like nor, during the painting process, what I am aiming at and what to do about getting there."[44]

Richter's biographer Dietmar Elger wrote,

> For Richter, the squeegee is the most important implement for integrating coincidence into his art. . . . the structure of paint applied with a squeegee can never be completely controlled . . . . Use of the squeegee thus places him in a situation where he does not have to actively create, but can observe as a paint structure comes into being on the canvas.[45]

Richter activates the material, which has a life of its own; then he decides when to stop and what to keep. In Richter's process, chance is situated between preparedness (such as either the development of a system, as in *Strip*, or the development of skill, as in the use of the squeegee in *Abstract Painting*) and judgement.

Richter first used a squeegee in 1980 with an oil-on-canvas painting simply entitled *Abstract Painting*.[46] However, this device did not immediately become the principal method of his abstract painting that it has become. Richter has spent years developing and perfecting this method designed to limit his own authorial control. Richter's oeuvre between 1980 and 1982 shows him experimenting with this method and testing the results. Many of these works lack the rich layering of material, form, and color that would come to exemplify Richter's subsequent abstracts.

---

[42] "Interview with Amine Hasse, 1982" in (Richter et al. 2009, p. 122).
[43] "I Have Nothing to Say and I'm Saying It." in (Godfrey et al. 2016, p. 27).
[44] Notes, 1985" in (Richter et al. 2009, p. 142).
[45] (Elger 2009, p. 251).
[46] Catalogue Raisonné: 456-1.

Richter's growing proficiency with this new tool is evidenced in works from 1982, such as *Oldenburg*,[47] *Yellow-Green*,[48] *Red*,[49] *Lilac*,[50] *Orangery*,[51] paintings that he exhibited at *Documenta 7*.[52] Richter's statement for the catalog of his participation in *Documenta 7* is perhaps the closest he has come to writing a manifesto for his painting.

He began by arguing for the importance of artificial models of reality, with the work of art being one type, perhaps the best type, of model. But without these models, he wrote, "we would know nothing of reality and would be animals."[53] This reflects Richter's earlier statement, "Picturing things . . . is what makes us human; art is making sense and giving shape to that sense. It is like the religious search for God. We are well aware that making sense and picturing are artificial, like illusion; but we can never give them up. For belief . . . is our most important characteristic."[54]

Richter continued his *Documenta 7* text writing, "Abstract pictures are fictive models, because they make visible a reality that we can neither see or describe, but whose existence we postulate."[55] Therefore, abstract painting not only creates a model of reality but of a reality beyond comprehension. And since this reality is beyond our natural comprehension, we struggle to attach words to it. "We denote this reality in negative terms: the unknown, the incomprehensible, the infinite. And for thousands of years we have been depicting it through surrogate images such as heaven and hell, gods and devils."[56]

Richter continued,

> In abstract painting we have found a better way of gaining access to the unvisualizable, the *incomprehensible*; because abstract painting deploys the utmost visual immediacy . . . in order to depict 'nothing' . . . . Instead we accept that we are seeing the unvisualizable: that which has never been seen before and is not visible.[57]

Richter concluded his *Documenta 7* catalog statement with the bold pronouncement, "Art is the highest form of hope."[58]

If Richter's hope is in an art that gains him, and the viewer, access to an incomprehensible and unvisualizable reality, the means to realize this art must also be beyond comprehension. The incomprehensible cannot, after all, be accessed through comprehensible means. In fact, while Richter's oeuvre has not been one of linear progression, there has been an arch of greater complexity. Initially, Richter used found photographs to limit his creative authorship, then he invented a tool that would allow him to more effectively incorporate chance into his process, and, most recently, he has used the computer to make creative choices, which he can accept or reject. Therefore, *Strip* and the *Strip Paintings* series are not entry of a painter into the realm of digital printmaking as much as a painting discovering how digital technology can function as a tool in his ongoing contest with his own creative impulse.

9. Chance

From *Abstract Painting*, to *Cathedral Window*, to *Strip*, Richter has employed artist-guided chance as a technique of visualizing the incomprehensible. In a 1990 interview, he explained his aim and strategy,

---

47 Catalogue Raisonné: 489.
48 Catalogue Raisonné: 492.
49 Catalogue Raisonné: 493.
50 Catalogue Raisonné: 494.
51 Catalogue Raisonné: 495.
52 *Documenta 7* was held 19 June and 28 October 1982, in Kassel, Germany.
53 "Text for catalog of *Documenta 7*, Kassel, 1982" in (Richter et al. 2009, p. 121).
54 "Notes, 1962" in (Richter et al. 2009, p. 14).
55 "Text for catalog of *documenta 7*, Kassel, 1982" in (Richter et al. 2009, p. 121).
56 "Text for catalog of *documenta 7*, Kassel, 1982" in (Richter et al. 2009, p. 121).
57 "Text for catalog of *documenta 7*, Kassel, 1982" in (Richter et al. 2009, p. 121). Italics added.
58 "Text for catalog of *documenta 7*, Kassel, 1982" in (Richter et al. 2009, p. 121).

I want to end up with a picture that I haven't planned. This method of arbitrary choice, chance, inspiration and destruction may produce a specific type of picture, but it never produces a predetermined picture. Each picture has to evolve out of a painterly or visual logic: it has to emerge as if inevitably.[59]

According to Richter, everything in life is coincidence. The existence of the universe in its present state is a coincidence. That Richter became a painter is coincidence. That Richter became a famous painter is coincidence. Nevertheless, human beings have creative compulsion, a desire to make something meaningful out of that accumulation of coincidences.

However, for Richter, chance is not meaningless absurdity; it is not automatism. To the contrary, structured chance is creative. In 1986, Richter said, "Above all, it's never blind chance: it's a chance that is always planned, but also always surprising. And I need it in order to carry on … to introduce something different and disruptive. I'm often astonished to find how much better chance is than I am."[60]

Richter noted that chance, guided by the artist's decisions, could be creative,

By accepting coincidence as an event that goes far beyond my faculties of imagination, even beyond all comprehension, I take on the role of someone who can only react to it—and yet, despite the helplessness of this position, can still make something out of it, to the point where it is no longer a coincidence any more.[61]

For Richter, chance is the revelation of nature's intellect, which is superior to human intellect or personal choice. Chance is a natural process. That is, nature works by and through chance. In nature, a seed becomes a tree, trees form a forest, by a process that is incalculable and cannot be predetermined. Created by a process that was thoroughly methodical, based on a series of premeditated steps, but that also involved an important element of guided chance, *Strip* demonstrates how rule-based chance can manifest an orderly design that is greater than the artist's own imagination.

10. Authorship Revisited

The process by which Richter created *Strip*, his use of photography, a computer, and artist-directed chance, all evidence his fundamental suspicion of artistic authorship.

The question of authorship and the authoritative voice of the artist has been one of the central concerns of Richter's art from the very beginning of his oeuvre.[62] To address his skepticism of authorship, Richter has frequently used conceptual schema to complicate his role as creative author. This can range from making a painting from a found photograph or a store-found color chart to using a computer to organize some 11,500 squares of colored glass for a window in Cologne Cathedral. And yet Richter's authorship continues to be present in the choices he makes, such as his selection of and, contrary to his statements, editing of the photographic image, his decision on when to begin and end the creative process.

Richter's skepticism of authorship, artistic authority, and originality, should, in part, be understood in the context of the climate of post-war German art. The most internationally famous German artist in the 1960s, when Richter was beginning his mature work, was Joseph Beuys. Beuys' creative production, which was comprised mainly of performances and the relics left over from performances, was premised on a cult of artistic personality that is perhaps unsurpassed in the history of art.

---

[59] "Interview with Sabine Schütz, 1990" in (Richter et al. 2009, p. 256).
[60] "Interview with *Benjamin* H.D. *Buchloh*" *in* (Richter et al. 2009, p. 182).
[61] Gerhard Richter quoted in "Paints and Layers: Abstract Paintings from 1986 to 2005" by Kerstin Küster in (Westheider and Philipp 2018, p. 173).
[62] Richter begins his self-created Catalogue Raisonné with works from 1962, even though he had created works before then. It could be argued that what differentiated these excluded works from those included in his Catalogue Raisonné was their approach to creative authorship.

To advance this doctrine of creative authenticity, Beuys employed a self-invented myth to mask his own personal history and present himself as a shaman healer. Following in the model of authoritative originally set by Beuys, younger artists, such as Georg Baselitz and Anselm Kiefer, began painting in an "authentically Germanic" method of heavily layered materials and gesturalism. These painters, collectively tagged with the Neo-Expressionist label, cultivated a Romantic conception of the work of art as a spiritual revelation of the artist's inner state of being.[63] Richter's embrace of impersonal methods, from appropriating deadpan photography to his reliance on chance, set him in a different direction from what was championed at the time, between the 1960s and 1980s, as the mainstream of German painting.[64] However, this strategy was not reactionary; Richter was deliberately improvising strategies that would complicate the issue of creative authorship.

Richter's suspicion of authorship is also, in part, grounded in his own technical dexterity. He was educated in a program, at the Dresden Art Academy, that emphasized traditional methods of drawing from plaster cast and human models. However, it seems that the more skilled he became, the less Richter trusted artistic talent. Technical skills only made it more possible for him to place himself in his own work.

Having achieved a high level of skill, he wanted methods that would short-circuit the emergence of a "signature style." Richter's refusal to work in any particular style is rooted in his belief that style is an expression of the artist. This idea of an artist having a signature style, something like the artist's handwriting, is bound up, at least in Richter's mind, with the idea of a work of art as the outpouring of the artist's inner being.

Richter's approach to painting is the opposite of an artist such as Wassily Kandinsky, for whose work Richter professes an antipathy.[65] For Kandinsky, the spiritual reality lay within the artist and the work of art was a means of making that inner reality materially visible. Richter rejects this notion of a spiritual reality within the artist waiting to find expression. For Richter, the artist is in the way of the material's own expression of itself. He said, "Pictures should be made according to a recipe. The act of making should occur without inner involvement, like crushing stones or painting a building."[66] His use of chance is a strategy of clearing himself away.

In "notes" written to himself in 1990, Richter wrote, "Accept that I can plan nothing."[67] He went on,

> Any thoughts on my part about the 'construction' of a picture are false, and if the execution works, this is only because I partially destroy it, or because it works in spite of everything—by not detracting and by not looking the way I planned.

> I often find this intolerable and even impossible to accept, because, as a thinking, planning human being, it humiliates me to find that I am so powerless. It casts doubt on my competence and any constructive ability. My only consolation is to tell myself that I did actually make the pictures—even though they are a law unto themselves, even though they treat me any way that they like and somehow just take shape.[68]

In an interview with Robert Storr, Richter claimed to be "clumsy" but he added that he has a good eye for judging bad and good art. For Richter, the capacity to decide, to say Yes or No to a manifestation, is the crux for his creativity.[69] Richter's solution to the problem of authorship is to

---

63   See (Cowart 1983).
64   Richter was not alone in his avoidance of Neo-Expressionism. He found artist kinship in Sigmar Polke, Blinky Palermo, and Konrad Lueg (later known by his real name Konrad Fischer).
65   (Storr 2003, p. 182).
66   (van Bruggen 1985, p. 86).
67   "Notes, 1990" in (Richter et al. 2009, p. 247).
68   "Notes, 1990" in (Richter et al. 2009, p. 247).
69   (Storr 2003, p. 161).

employ artist-directed chance. He uses chance to get beyond himself, to reach something greater than himself, something unknown.

However, Richter's doubts should not be confused with ambivalence. He cares and believes deeply. He acts with a sense of purpose. But this sense of purpose is balanced by a skepticism of the result. He is skeptical if the result will be successful. In fact, the success of the work of art for Richter might be if it can succeed in overcoming the artist's skepticism. Richter's much-celebrated doubt is not an end in and of itself. It is his safeguard against a false sense of success. This is not a doubt in the possibility of success, just the certainty that success will not come easily within the limits of human facility. In notes written to himself, Richter wrote, "Of course I constantly despair at my own incapacity, at the impossibility of ever accomplishing anything, of painting a valid, true picture or even knowing what such a thing ought to look like, But then I always have the hope that, if I persevere, it might one day happen."[70]

11. Painting Like Nature

Richter has placed his hope in the possibility that a more perfect painting might be created by nature, by the process of painting itself rather than being guided by his hand. Artist-guided chance, either through the squeegee tool or some other process, solved one problem in Richter's art in that it seems to have satisfied his desire for equilibrium between fortuitous accident and creative control. Through rule-structured chance, Richter wants to create a work of art that exceeds what a human can make through intention, expression, or technique. However, this process of working by chance also created a new problem. Richter noted, "Using chance is painting like nature—but which chance event, out of all the countless possibilities."[71]

If he is working by chance, how does Richter know when his painting is finished? According to Richter, "Consciously, I can't calculate the result. But subconsciously, I can sense it."[72]

In his 1990 "notes," Richter wrote,

> ... it's still up to me to determine the point at which they are finished (picture-making consists of a multitude of Yes/No decisions and a Yes decision to end it all). If I look at it that way, the whole thing starts to seem quite natural again—or rather nature-like, [the work of art is] alive ... [73]

This reference to nature is significant. It goes to the question, "how does Gerhard Richter know when a painting is 'finished'?" In the documentary *Gerhard Richter: Painting*, which documents him working in the studio over a period of months, the continually present problem is how to know when a work of art is ready to leave the studio and live in the world.

Richter said, "I believe that art has a kind of rightness, as in music, when we hear whether or not a note is false. And that is why the old classical pictures, which are right in their own terms, are so necessary for me. In addition to that there's nature, which I see also has this rightness."[74]

There are two terms from Richter's statement that need further explanation, "classical pictures" and "rightness."

In an interview with Robert Storr, Richter said, "True classical art—as distinct from conservative classical or neoclassical style—may be defined as an art that accepts its own conventions but does not simply repeat them formulaically. Rather it uses them to transform itself and extend its range."[75]

---

[70] "Notes, 1985" in (Richter et al. 2009, p. 140).

[71] "Notes, 1985" in (Richter et al. 2009, p. 140). In her essay, "'Painting like nature': Chance and the Landscape in Gerhard Richter's Overpainted Photographs", Aline Guillermet points out that the translation in *Text* incorrectly reads: 'Using chance is like painting nature' whereas the German reads: 'Den Zufall nützen ist, wie die Natur abmalen'. (Guillermet 2017, p. 198)

[72] (Elger 2009, p. 251).

[73] "Notes, 1990" in (Richter et al. 2009, p. 247).

[74] (van Bruggen 1985, p. 82).

[75] (Storr 2003, p. 182).

Richter continued, "A crucial dimension of such classical art, though, is that it is deeply impersonal. Pollock, when he painted the big allover abstractions of the late 1940s and early 1950s, was for perhaps the first time of his life free of himself as a painter and thoroughly involved with the paint and the space and the process. In that sense, his was a classical art."[76]

So, by "classical painting" Richter means one of the most controversial artists of the 20th century, the Abstract Expressionist Jackson Pollock. This is an insightful point that needs to be returned to, but first, we need to look at the meaning of Richter's concept of "rightness."

In a 1987 interview with Anna Tilroe, Richter said, "I believe I am looking for rightness. My work has so much to do with reality that I wanted to have a corresponding rightness. That excludes painting in imitation. In nature, everything is always right: the structure is right, the proportions are good, the colors fit the forms. If you imitate that in painting, it becomes false."[77]

It is interesting that Richter finds the same "rightness" in both a classical work of art and nature. He is not more specific about what constitutes this "rightness" but, it seems to me, this is the goal of his art. When is a painting done? When it has reached "rightness" or an approximation of "rightness."

But how does a painter reach "rightness"? This brings us back to the work of Pollock and Richter's definition of "classical painting." In a statement entitled "My Painting," Pollock described the process by which he created the allover paintings that Richter admired as "classical." He wrote,

> When I am *in* my painting, I'm not aware of what I'm doing. It is only after a sort of "get acquainted" period that I see what I have been about. I have no fears about making changes, destroying the image, etc. because the painting has a life of its own. I try to let it come through. It is only when I lose contact with the painting that the result is a mess. Otherwise there is pure harmony, an easy give and take, and the painting comes out well.[78]

Pollock's statement shares a conceptual kinship with Richter's own 1990 pronouncement that his art is created through a process that is beyond himself, a process that he can only shape through the acceptance or rejection of each unplanned outcome.

In an interview with Nicholas Serota, Richter described the motivation for his persistence in painting, in a period over fifty years, as "a desire to maintain a certain artistic quality that moves us, that goes beyond what we are, and that is, in that sense timeless."[79]

12. Skepticism as a Form of Belief

Gerhard Richter's writings, interviews, and, most significantly, his art evidence a fundamental skepticism of all received knowledge, including artistic, philosophical, political, and religious teachings. In notes dated from 1962, which are the earliest notes in his collected writings, Richter writes, "There is no excuse whatever for uncritically accepting what one take over from others."[80] However, in the very next paragraph, he states,

> Picturing things, taking a view is what makes us human; art is making sense and giving shape to that sense. It is like a religious search for God. We are well aware that making sense and picturing are artificial, like illusion; but we can never give them up. For belief (thinking out and interpreting the present and the future) is our most important characteristic.[81]

These statements of doubt and faith are not incongruous; they inform each other.

---

[76] (Storr 2003, p. 182).
[77] (Storr 2003, p. 198).
[78] Jackson Pollock "My Painting." First published in *Possibilities* (Winter 1947–1948) pp. 78–83. Reprinted in (Karmel 2002, p. 18). Italics Pollock's.
[79] (Godfrey et al. 2016, p. 15).
[80] (Elger 2009, p. 14).
[81] (Elger 2009, p. 14).

Richter's position echoes that of Marcel Duchamp, whom he greatly admires, when Duchamp, in a filmed interview with James Johnson Sweeney, stated,

> I like the word "belief." I think, in general, when people say "I know," they don't know, they believe .... I believe that art is the form of activity in which man, as man, shows himself to be a true individual and is capable of going beyond the animal state. Because art is an outlet toward regions which are not ruled by time and space.

Then, with a smile, Duchamp concluded, "To live is to believe. That is my belief."[82] Like Duchamp, Richter is skeptical of "knowing" but finds hope in "belief."

Strip is one of the most recent, and arguably one of the most successful, manifestations of a central theme in Gerhard Richter's art, namely the persistent and unfulfilled longing to believe in something larger or greater than himself. His hope of possibly realizing this indefinable purpose prevents this longing from becoming melancholia. Richter's art both visualizes this longing and, by giving material form to this longing, fulfills it, at least in part. And this work of art gives Richter hope that this longing will one day find fulfillment.

In an interview with Benjamin Buchloh, Richter suggested that his art was an expression of longing. To this, Buchloh incredulously asked "Longing for what?" Richter responded "For lost qualities, for a better world—for the opposite of misery and hopelessness." He added, "I might also call it redemption."[83] Buchloh, who has consistently denied the possibility of the expression of the spiritual in art, changed the subject. However, as an artist, an immensely talented artist, Richter has an awareness of creating something that is more than he imagined. He finds hope, even redemption, in the reality that the work of art can have an indefinable presence that is greater than the sum of its material elements. The work of art has something that the artist didn't put there.

In a paradoxical oeuvre of elusive beauty and agnostic romanticism, Richter's *Strip Paintings* are among his most conceptually complex and visually intoxicating works. These prints begin from a foundation of skepticism and, through a process of calculated accidents, arrive at a state of material presence that is somewhere beyond belief.

If the work of art models a method of looking at, thinking about, and acting in the world, Richter's *Strip* encourages the viewer to embrace the inconceivable and to creatively turn the coincidences of life into beauty. Our awareness of ourselves, of our place in the world, and of our as-yet realized potential is expanded by *Strip*. The digital print makes us more fully human.

In 1989, Richter told an interviewer, "I don't believe in the absolute picture. There can only be approximations, experiments, and beginnings, over and over."[84] But in 2002, he told Storr, "A painting can help us to think something that goes beyond this senseless existence. That's something art can do."[85] These statements evidence an optimistic skepticism that is manifested in both the process that created *Abstract Painting* and then *Strip* as well as the visual experience of measureless beauty that we find in these works.

The *Strip Paintings* series represents, in my opinion, the most significant new development in Gerhard Richter's oeuvre since he began using the squeegee three decades ago. If Richter, in turn, is regarded as one of the most important painters working today, then the *Strip Paintings* series are an important development in the state of contemporary art.

Strip is not likely to be the end of Richter's explorations into the relationship between artist-guided chance and creative authorship. Nor is this series of unique prints likely to be Richter's last endeavor into the realm of the incomprehensible. In 1962, the year that he began his mature work, Richter made notes to himself, saying, "Strange though this may sound, not knowing where one is going—being

---

[82] (Sweeney 1956).
[83] "Interview with Benjamin H.D. Buchloh" in (Richter et al. 2009, p. 181).
[84] "Conversation with Jan-Thorn Prikker concerning the 18 October 1977 cycle, 1989" in (Richter et al. 2009, p. 235).
[85] "MoMA Interview with Robert Storr" in (Richter et al. 2009, p. 431).

lost, being a loser—reveals the greatest possible faith and optimism, as against collective security and collective significance. To believe, one must have lost God; to paint, one must have lost art."[86] Six decades later, Richter's search has gained focus, vigor, and intensity but he finds creative exhilaration in the prospect that it has come no closer to resolution.

Funding: This research received no external funding.

Conflicts of Interest: The author declares no conflict of interest.

References

Belz, Corinna. 2012. *Gerhard Richter Painting*. DVD. Berlin: Zero One Film.

Buchloh, Benjamin H. D. 2012. *Gerhard Richter: Strip Paintings*. New York: Marian Goodman Gallery.

Cowart, Jack. 1983. *Expressions: New Art from Germany: Georg Baselitz, Jörg Immendorff, Anselm Kiefer, Markus Lüpertz, A.R. Penck*. Munich: Prestel-Verlag in Association with the Saint Louis Art Museum.

Elger, Dietmar. 2009. *Gerhard Richter: A Life in Painting*. Chicago: University of Chicago Press.

Guillermet, Aline. 2017. 'Painting like nature': Chance and the Landscape in Gerhard Richter's Overpainted Photographs. *Art History* 40: 178–99. [CrossRef]

Godfrey, Mark, Dorothée Brill, Camille Morineau, Achim Borchardt-Hume, Rachel Haidu, Christine Mehring, and Nicholas Serota. 2016. *Gerhard Richter: Panorama: A Retrospective*. Expanded ed. London: Tate Publishing.

Karmel, Pepe. 2002. *Jackson Pollock: Key Interviews, Articles, and Reviews*. New York: The Museum of Modern Art.

Storr, Robert. 2003. *Gerhard Richter. Doubt and Belief in Painting*. New York: The Museum of Modern Art.

Richter, Gerhard, Dietmar Elger, and Hans Ulrich Obrist. 2009. *Text: Writings, Interviews and Letters: 1961–2007*. London: Thames and Hudson.

Richter, Gerhard. 2012. *Gerhard Richter: Patterns: Divided, Mirrored, Repeated*. New York: D.A.P./Distributed Art Publishers.

Romaine, James. 2009. Gerhard Richter: The Capacity for Belief. *Image* 64: 43–56.

Sweeney, James Johnson. 1956. Marcel Duchamp, Interview on Art and Dada. Available online: https://www.youtube.com/watch?v=DzwADsrOEJk&t=2s (accessed on 16 April 2019).

van Bruggen, Coosje. 1985. Gerhard Richter: Painting as a Moral Act. *Artforum International* 9: 82–91.

Westheider, Ortrud, and Michael Philipp, eds. 2018. *Gerhard Richter: Abstraction*. Munich: Prestel.

---

[86] "Notes, 1962" in (Richter et al. 2009, p. 15).

Essay

Aesthetic Experience as a Spiritual Support of *Homo Post-Secularis*

Victor Bychkov

RAS Institute of Philosophy, Goncharnaya St. 12/1, 109240 Moscow, Russia; vbychkov48@yandex.ru

Received: 13 February 2019; Accepted: 2 April 2019; Published: 4 April 2019

Abstract: The essay begins with an analysis of the cultural situation of humanity after its transition to secular mentality and a gradual disenchantment with secularism, which leads to the formation of post-secular mentality. It further suggests that aesthetic experience traditionally served as a bridge between the secular and the religious/spiritual and can serve in this capacity again in the post-secular age. It outlines the main traits of the post-secular person (homo post-saecularis). Two aspects of aesthetic experience are emphasized: its in-depth penetration into nature in an attempt to achieve unity with it, and the aesthetic observation of artworks. In pursuing both of these aspects, the post-secular person attempts, just as Romantics and Symbolists previously, to grasp something invisible beyond visible forms and escape from banal reality into higher spiritual realms of being, ultimately experiencing him- or herself as having a place in the universe. Aesthetic experience, if it is correctly understood and practiced, can give all this to the present-day post-secular person. The rest of the essay is devoted to a brief history of twentieth-century views of art, mainly in French and Russian thought, that foreshadow its post-secular role, and to the author's authentic theoretical framework for understanding art and aesthetic experience, as well as his, equally authentic, program of how to achieve the post-secular function of art in practice for a present-day person.

Keywords: culture; faith; secularism; aesthetic experience; wonder; art; beauty; theurgy

1. Culture and *Post*-Culture

The past century and a half has been marked by a turbulent, if not explosive, movement of all cultural and civilizational processes that have affected the spiritual world of the human being. By the middle of the twentieth century, Culture with the capital "C" (high culture) has been replaced by *post*-culture. Culture, as I understand it, stands for a period that spans many thousands of years, during which humanity developed under the sign of faith in the existence of the Great Other (the God of monotheism for the Judaeo-Christian cultures of the most recent times). During the period of the Renaissance, this faith began to weaken; secularized culture took over and, approximately by the middle of the past century, the creative segment of "Western" humanity, in both Europe and the New World, entered the period of *post*-culture. This segment of human kind rejects faith in God and assumes a faith in scientific-technological progress, which is, from its point of view, the only worthy aspect of our civilization. At this point in time, *homo saecularis*—a group of creative and talented people (above all, in the areas of natural sciences and technology)—reach the high point of their development and continue to show off their superiority over the remaining part of humanity.

At the same time, traditional religiosity still exists in rather large groups of European and New World populations. However, in the overwhelming majority of these populations, religiosity has withered into formal ritualism, and the spiritual-mystical foundation of traditional religions, which also served as the foundation of high Culture, has disappeared. Today, a trip to a church is purely habitual: our parents used to go, the majority of the neighbors go, and it feels awkward not to go. So, in reality, even this layer of the population already belongs to *post*-culture. People of deep faith have

Religions **2019**, *10*, 250

not determined the spiritual atmosphere of the inhabitants of Europe and European settlers around the globe since the mid-twentieth century (if not from the early 1900s). Imperceptibly, Culture has been replaced by civilization, which has scientific-technological progress for a king or god, and the Humanities are dominated by the ironizing tone of postmodernism.[1]

However, it is not that easy to believe in the results of the relentless stream of scientific-technological discoveries as in something exclusively positive. The radical secularism of *post*-culture has led humanity to an anthropological crisis, which one feels sharply both in religion and, more broadly, within the scientific-technological civilization itself. Human beings have lost their link to their deep spiritual roots. It is not by chance that as far back as the middle of the past century many prominent scientists in leading branches of natural sciences and technologies began to sound an alarm. They realized that the path that scientific development had taken can cause catastrophic consequences for humanity, for the humanistically oriented public began to lose control over many areas of scientific-technological research.[2] These warnings have been heeded by a rather wide circle of people worldwide. The enthusiasm for the supposedly salvific function of scientific-technological progress has significantly lessened. Enter the age of *homo postsaecularis*.

2. A Dialog between Religious and Secular Mentalities

Presently, there are different concepts of the postsecular.[3] First, after a dialog of sorts at the threshold between the past and present centuries between, on the one hand, Jürgen Habermas, who rejected radical atheism, and on the other hand, pope John Paul II, who paid a special attention to the interrelation of faith and reason,[4] postsecularism is conceptualized as a dialog and a tendency toward mutual understanding between the religious and secular mentalities, which could be mutually enriching. This path is not straight-forward, and therefore, in my opinion, aesthetic experience can become, on the one hand, one of the important ways of containing radical secularism, and on the other hand, one of the conduits of the postsecular worldview. In fact, it is precisely aesthetic experience that has served as a bridge between religious faith and secular mentality since secularism made its appearance during the time of the Renaissance. At least until the mid-twentieth century, both believers of various confessions and the secular public readily perceived art (which is the concentrated form of existence of aesthetic experience) as a significant spiritual phenomenon.

Together with this idea of postsecularism, we are also familiar with the postsecular person. The postsecular person basically rejects traditional religiosity of any kind and traditional gods, including the Christian God—although, perhaps, still habitually attending traditional liturgies. At the same time, the postsecular person has not lost faith in the high spiritual principle and is in search of a path towards it. Today, the search follows two directions: neo-religious (the search for and creation of new religious forms of ascent to the Absolute) and completely non-religious, in the traditional sense of religiosity. It is precisely following the latter direction that the mid-twentieth-century predecessor of the postsecular person had faith in the progress and salvific mission of science—however, the postsecular person has rejected even that faith.

---

[1] Translation from Russian by Oleg Bychkov. See more on the spiritual and aesthetic aspects of postmodernism in Mankovskaya 2016b.

[2] The well-known *Humanist manifestos* of prominent scientists and public figures of the past century (the Humanist Manifestos of 1933, 1973, 2003; the most complete manifesto appeared in 2000 under the aegis of the Council for Secular Humanism [Kurtz 2000]) call upon humanity to refocus the efforts of our civilization on human beings, their life and well-being, but seldom is scientific research aimed in this direction.

[3] On the concept and origin of the postsecular as relevant to the topic of the present essay, see Warner et al. 2010; Taylor 2011; Bennett 2001.

[4] See Habermas 2006 and the encyclical *Fides et Ratio*, 14 September 1998, http://w2.vatican.va/content/john-paul-ii/en/encyclicals/documents/hf_jp-ii_enc_14091998_fides-et-ratio.html.

3. Aesthetic Experience as a Path

The postsecular person's search for spirituality is associated exclusively with a new understanding of the phenomenon of life itself and with non-utilitarian forms of contact with life, its origins, and cosmo-anthropic being. Here, we see the increasing role of the phenomenon of *wonder*, which, notably, is also present in aesthetic experience.[5] Therefore, one of the main directions in the search for postsecular spirituality could be the contemporary person's renewed interest in the area of aesthetic experience;[6] in its two main aspects: (1) its in-depth penetration into nature and its pursuit of unity with nature; and (2) aesthetic contemplation of art works. Pursuing both of these aspects of aesthetic experience, the contemporary person, just as the Romantics and Symbolists did previously, attempts to grasp something invisible beyond visible forms, to escape into higher spiritual realms of being from day-to-day reality, and finally to feel like human beings have their place in the Universe. If the contemporary postsecular person correctly understands and practices aesthetic experience, it can provide him or her with all this.

At this point it is worth recalling that during the period of the waning of religiosity and spread of secularism at the end of the nineteenth century, there were lively discussions about the high spiritual potential of art among the French Symbolists. One of their spiritual masterminds, Joséphin (Sâr) Péladan, felt the crisis and decay of religious consciousness sharply. Art and religion, he claimed, had the same divine origin and, therefore during the period of spiritual decay, art could replace religion: "Art is the last form of religiosity during periods of decay; if it is extinguished, putrefaction accelerates" (Péladan 1898, p. 96). Péladan was convinced that art and aesthetics led the human being toward the same ideals and the same God as religion; however, in the contemporary world, artistic experience is foregrounded. In an anti-religious atmosphere, "those who no longer enter churches frequent museums", where they search for "sacred emotions", for the "ideal", "mystical", and "lyric" (Péladan 1905, p. 91). During the period of expectation of the coming of the Holy Spirit—i.e., his own period, according to Péladan—art and beauty become the most important ways to God. According to the contemporary scholar of Péladan's thought, Nadya Mankovskaya, he "sets the goal of restoring the lost (so he thought) knowledge and ideals of Catholicism. *Tradition* will serve as the foundation of this restoration; *art* will serve as its platform; and *beauty* will be its means. Beauty that is expressed in works of art is capable of leading humanity to God and preparing the coming of the Holy Spirit. True art is charged with the divine mission of elevating the human soul" (Mankovskaya 2016a, p. 82). During the period of the rise of secular tendencies, Péladan's pathos is quite understandable. In the beginning of the twentieth century, the aspirations of the Russian Symbolists, such as Andrei Belyi, Vyacheslav Ivanov, and others, were close to those of Péladan. They were developing the theory of theurgy, which amounted to art transcending its traditional boundaries and becoming part of real life in order to co-create it together with God according to aesthetic laws.

4. Theurgy

In ancient times, the term 'theurgy' signified sacred and mystical communication between chosen individuals and the divine world in the process of special ritual actions, with the resulting acquisition of secret knowledge from the gods. Vladimir Soloviev, a Russian philosopher of the late 1800s, conceptualizes theurgy as the ancient "substantial unity of creative activity, which is consumed by mysticism," whose essence lies in the unity of earthly and heavenly elements in the process of sacred creativity. In particular, he singles out the contemporary stage of theurgy, which he designates as "free theurgy" or "holistic creativity". He sees its essence in conscious and mystical "communication

---

[5]   On the concept of wonder, especially as relevant to aesthetics, see: Costa 2011; Vasalou 2015; Willmott 2018; Levine 2006.

[6]   Today, more and more frequently one hears voices in favor of giving aesthetic experience and aesthetics as a discipline a higher rank in human cultural hierarchy compared to the past centuries. For example, Wolfgang Welsch thinks that, today, aesthetics is turning into a "universal philosophy" (Welsch 1996).

with the heavenly world by means of inner creative activity", which is based on the organic unity of the principal constitutive elements of creativity: mysticism, "fine art", and "technical artistry" (Soloviev 1966, p. 286). This sort of understanding of theurgy and theurgic creativity resonated both with the Symbolists and with many Russian religious thinkers at the beginning of the twentieth century. Poet Vyacheslav Ivanov specifically focuses on Soloviev's idea that the art of the future must freely establish a new link with religion, when artists (theurges) themselves will consciously control "earthly realizations" of the religious idea. According to Ivanov, theurges, as bearers of divine revelation, are true creators of myth and symbolists in the highest sense, and theurgy is the "action that is imprinted with the seal of God's Name" (Ivanov 1974, p. 646). Although theurgy has not been realized in its full sense, it is precisely theurgy that inspires the Russian Symbolists in their creative activity.

As the highest stage of creative activity, theurgy, which is understood as life itself as assisted by the divine energy of Sophia, the Wisdom of God, and the original Symbol itself (Christ), is also very important to Andrei Belyi. He discerns "pursuit of theurgy" in Nietzsche's wisdom and considers Vladimir Soloviev's statement about the "joining of the heights of symbolism as art with mysticism" as the most precise definition of the essence of theurgy (Belyi 1994, p. 218). Human creativity at its height consists, to use Belyi's terminology, of three ascending "acts". The first act is the creation of a world of the arts. The second act is the "creation of oneself in the image and likeness of the world"—i.e., perfecting oneself—which happens in the process of a vigorous struggle against one's inert "I", or the "guardian of the threshold", who blocks one's access to the kingdom of freedom. Here, a tragic discord resounds within a person when the artist leaves his or her art. The third (future) act is the entrance of persons into the kingdom of freedom and the "new link between unconditionally free people for the purpose of creating a community of life in the image and likeness of the new names that have been secretly inscribed in us by the Spirit" (Belyi 1994, p. 465). It is precisely this final act that, according to Belyi, corresponds to the level of theurgic creativity (or existence) that is founded on an inspiration from above.

The idea of theurgy is developed in Nikolai Berdyaev's book, *Smysl tvorchestva. Opyt opravdaniia cheloveka* (*The Meaning of Creativity. The Experience of the Justification of the Human Being*, 1916): "Theurgy is the kind of art that creates another world, another existence, another life, beauty as something existent. Theurgy overcomes the tragedy of creative act and directs creative energy at the new life". Theurgy puts an end to all traditional art and literature, all division of creativity; it completes traditional culture as a product of human effort and begins "superculture," for "theurgy is human action together with God—or God-action, a creativity of God-Man " (Berdyaev 1985, p. 283).[7]

Contemporary reality so far has given us no reason to get our hopes up as far as the symbolist and theurgic ideals are concerned. However, the aspirations of symbolists and theurgists to secure a position of prominence for art in spiritual culture during the period of secularization should make us pay close attention to art even now: after all, art has functioned in Culture at the same time as and in complete harmony with religion. And, even today, art can give us much more than mere wonder and amazement.

5. Art as a Postsecular Phenomenon

Therefore, in what follows, I would like to provide a more detailed account of art as the quintessence of aesthetic experience as a whole, which promises new spiritual perspectives to the contemporary person. On the basis of the experience of the previous generations, *homo postsaecularis* intuitively feels that one can reach spiritual heights by way of mastering and experiencing high art. As a rule, however, they do not know nor care to articulate what *exactly* this experience provides for them. Therefore, we remind ourselves here of the metaphysical foundations of art (upon which, as a matter of fact, all world religions have leaned from time immemorial).

---

[7] See in more detail in Bychkov 2007, pp. 489–575, 703–11.

So what is art as far as its essential foundations are concerned? At present, we can provide a more or less articulate answer to this question on the basis of the almost three-hundred-year period of existence of aesthetics as a discipline, which has been mostly devoted to searching for an answer to this notoriously difficult question.

Art is an *event*.

It is an event that is tremendously important and vital for the human being. It is not an accident that art, together with rudimentary forms of religion, appeared at the very dawn of the existence of *homo sapiens* as a species and remained with us over the entire period of our history.

The main significance of this event is that, in it, the *aesthetic experience of the human being* and humanity as whole is *expressed and manifested* in a concentrated form during particular periods of human history. It appears that this experience, as well as religious experience (it is not an accident either that the two have been intertwined since times immemorial), has participated, over many thousands of years, in the formation of the human being, of the human psyche, its mentality, and Culture itself.

(I should like to note, as an aside, that aesthetic experience should not be reduced merely to art; it permeates almost all aspects of human life. However, in this particular case, we speak of art where aesthetic experience is expressed in a concentrated form; essentially, art appeared in order to express this type of experience.)

The essence of *aesthetic experience* as far as art is concerned, i.e., the *essence of art itself*, can be reduced to several key functions:

1. The entire system of artistic devices *expresses* certain *meanings* that are vital to human beings. These meanings in principle *cannot be verbalized*; they cannot be expressed or grasped by the human being in any other way. This method of expression rests on *artistic images and symbols*, which constitute *artistic language*.

2. At the instant of aesthetic perception, art thereby performs an *anagogical* function by lifting human beings from their day-to-day life and elevating them into other, higher worlds. This is accomplished by means of immersing them into *artistic space*.

3. Art contributes to creating *harmony*: within the human being; between the human being and society; and even between the human being and the Universe as a whole. Art thereby induces a feeling of *fullness of being*, of one's participation in this fullness, and therefore of one's self-worth in the Universe. ('The Universe' here stands for the cosmoanthropic whole, within which the human being exists.) This fullness of being means that, with the help of art and through art, human beings are really plugged into the cosmoanthropic creative process and feel themselves as equal partners in it.

4. Finally, art is one of the principal conveyers of one of the most important values: *beauty*. By and large, artworks from times immemorial were cherished precisely for their beauty (or, to use current parlance, for their *aesthetic quality*). It is well known that it is precisely beauty that many eighteenth-century philosophers considered the subject of aesthetics. Charles Batteux, a French thinker and rhetorician, even introduced the term *les beaux arts* (lit. "beautiful arts") to describe art as an aesthetic phenomenon, i.e., to express the essence of art. And it is in this sense that the arts were understood, both in aesthetics and in habitual references to the arts, until the middle of the twentieth century.

In many respects, art performs all of its principal aforesaid functions (*expressive of vital meanings, anagogical, harmonizing*) precisely thanks to the fact that it both *expresses* and *creates* this value, i.e., thanks to its *axiological* function.

It is quite clear and commonly known that, historically, art did not seem to have emerged in order to actualize this value. Almost always, art has performed most important non-aesthetic functions in Culture: religious, political, social, ethical, narrative, etc. It is first of all for these reasons that art has been highly valued in society and paid for by clients.

6. The Aesthetic Essence of Art

However, art has been able to perform all these other functions exclusively with the help of its *aesthetic nature*. It is only high-quality (i.e., highly aesthetic) art that was capable—by purely artistic means—of effectively performing those non-artistic functions that society assigned to it. Therefore, the *high artistic* (read: *aesthetic*) *quality* of the artwork is its *essential* characteristic. It is clear that historically not everybody, and not always (and for the most time hardly anybody and infrequently), understood why art functioned so effectively in religion, politics, and so forth. At the same time, most felt very strongly that it would be difficult to manage those areas of culture without the support of art, no matter how unclear the reasons of its effectiveness were. It is precisely for this reason that, from ancient times onward, art has been so tightly wedded to religious practices all across the world. Moreover, those historical forms of art that we have known from time immemorial all the way to the mid-twentieth century *have been created by human beings with religious mentalities, who believed in the existence of the Great Other, or God*. One would be well advised not to ignore this fundamental fact when one thinks about the essence of art today.

Now, this *high artistic quality*, i.e., the aesthetic "matter" of art, is so subtle and beyond the grasp of reason that humanity is yet to say something convincing about it despite persistent attempts to understand this quality throughout time. This is all the more surprising given that this high artistic quality of artworks is strongly felt intuitively—and with some degree of agreement—within communities of professional artists, art critics, and aestheticians, i.e., people with a highly developed aesthetic taste who are steeped in aesthetic experience on a regular basis.

However, let us return to my definition of art as an *event*.

Is Leonardo's *Gioconda* that simply hangs on a wall in the Louvre not art? No, it is not.

I call art an event precisely because it is a specific, *unique process of communication* between the recipient, the artwork, and something else that stands *behind* the latter.

7. The Event of Art

In order to realize the event of art fully, four critical components are required.

1. An artwork of high artistic quality.
2. A recipient or subject of perception of art who is *aesthetically prepared*.
3. A *stance* to perceive this artwork precisely *aesthetically*, and not in any other way.
4. *Conditions* that are conducive of the realization of this perception.

Beginning with ancient times (at a theoretical level, with Aristotle and Longinus) and until (more or less) the middle of the twentieth century, few people who had any connection to art doubted the first requirement. An artwork must possess a number of *objective characteristics*, which can trigger a process of *aesthetic* perception of the work in a recipient. (Not all of these characteristics—such as [to take painting as an example] certain color combinations, visual rhythms, compositional relations, etc.—can be verbalized, but they are distinctly felt by an aesthetically trained eye and ear.).

It is another matter that the availability of highly artistic work is totally insufficient for an event of art to occur. For example, if a religious pilgrim prostrates himself before Andrei Rublyov's icon of the Trinity exhibited in the Tretyakov Gallery in Moscow and attempts to kiss it, no event of art has taken place here. For this pilgrim, the icon of the great iconographer is merely an object of religious veneration, and does not represent an aesthetic value. Alternatively, if an art dealer poses in front of a Corot and begins to evaluate the price of this canvas, no event of art has taken place here either. The artwork functions here merely as an object of commerce.

Therefore, in order for an event of art to occur, perhaps the most important requirement is the second: an availability of a subject who is *aesthetically prepared*. This means that an artwork is engaged by a person who possesses a rather developed *aesthetic taste* and is proficient, to a certain extent, in the *artistic language* of the type of art that she is about to appreciate.

Let us recall that the category of *taste* was introduced into aesthetics in the eighteenth century in order to designate the human *faculty* that perceives the beautiful—or, to broaden the category, aesthetic values. According to Kant, it is precisely the faculty of taste that performs (non-verbal!) *aesthetic judgments* (including judgments of artworks) on the basis of the feelings of *pleasure* or *displeasure*. The eighteenth-century greats all but exhausted the subject of taste, and the main aspects of their understanding of taste remain relevant even today.

The presence of taste, certainly, is the principal and most crucial requirement in the subject of aesthetic perception. However, a *knowledge base* of the peculiar artistic languages of different historical periods, ethnic groups, and types of art is also essential. One must study these languages by perusing expert literature, attending specialist lectures, but first of all by *engaging* actual artworks *regularly*. This is because this type of knowledge is of a special kind: it is non-discursive, practically impossible to articulate, but is acquired in the process of training one's perception while perceiving actual artworks.

For people who do not possess a particular level of taste and are not trained to engage specific types of art, i.e., for those who do not "know" (intuitively) the language of art, *art does not exist*. To be sure, they look at an artwork—this is the purpose of their visit, after all!—but they *do not see* it, and no event of art happens in this case.

The last two requirements—a *stance* to perceive an artwork *aesthetically*, and conditions that are *conducive* of the realization of aesthetic perception—are, of course, also important. It is essential that the subject come to a museum, concert hall, or theater with this sort of *stance*. For example, it is important that he perceive Surikov's "Lady Morozova" as a work of the *art of painting*, and not as an illustration from the life of a well-known Old Believer.

Aesthetic perception also requires certain favorable external *conditions* of perception. These are particularly difficult to provide these days in famous museums that contain artistic masterpieces, each of which is surrounded by a large crowd of selfie enthusiasts eager to take a picture. An event of art will hardly happen successfully for a subject of aesthetic perception under such conditions. He will gaze with sadness over the heads of the selfie-taking crowd at the same *Gioconda* and move on to adjacent galleries, where one could find less famous, but no less aesthetically valuable artworks. There, he will immerse himself fully in their perception, which requires a rather long and quiet period of *contemplation*.

The *main indicator* of an occurrence of an *event of art* is spiritual joy and *aesthetic pleasure*, which the recipient experiences in the process of perception and *contemplation* of an artwork (the latter constitutes the principal stage of aesthetic perception). This pleasure is precisely an *indicator*, and not the end of the aesthetic perception of art (or of anything else). However, most recipients do not understand such theoretical subtleties and often crave to experience artworks precisely for the sake of this pleasure, which was recognized as early as in ancient Greek thought.

To sum up what has been said, one can provide one of the currently possible definitions of art as an aesthetic event that immerses the contemporary person into the spiritual depths of being.

Art is an *event* (in the sense of "happening") of an expression (which is most fully given in history and perceptible by the senses) of aesthetic experience; this event is most fully realized in the spiritual world of a subject who has been prepared *aesthetically* and has a *stance* to perceive an object aesthetically; this subject is adequately *situated* to perceive *artistically significant* artworks. The latter include works that have been created following the principles of *imagistic-symbolic representation or expression* of any reality (metaphysical, spiritual, natural, material, artificial, social, psychic, etc.) and that help the recipient to plumb the *depths of meaning* of the reality that is being expressed, of the object that is being represented, or of the artwork itself—the depths that are inaccessible by any other means of cognition and that often extend far beyond the limits of what is being represented or the images that are used to represent it. In the course of this event, the recipient *acquires new knowledge*, is *elevated* to alternative levels of being beyond our day-to-day existence, and is ideally *harmonized* with the Universe and feels the fullness of being. The *aesthetic pleasure* that the recipient experiences serves as a witness to the realization of the event of art.

If one understands and treats art—and, broadly speaking, aesthetic experience as a whole—in this way, it becomes, perhaps, the most adequate and effective way of elevating the contemporary person to the highest rungs of the spiritual world. It is clear from what has been said, that in order to have proper aesthetic experience—especially the experience of art—the recipient must spend many years and apply a considerable spiritual effort preparing for it, constantly honing their spiritual (aesthetic, in this case) abilities. There is nothing unexpected here. The proper way to have a spiritual experience requires this sort of preparation and training. However, unlike other spiritual disciplines, aesthetic experience in culture remains the most universal, accessible, and historically possessed—to some extent and in some elementary form, which can always be developed further—by the majority of average people. And the postsecular person's yearning to develop this experience in themselves is still strongly felt even today.

8. Contemporary Art Practices

It is another matter that contemporary art, which alone claims to be relevant today, provides virtually no opportunity for an aesthetically sensitive person to have an aesthetic experience. For the most part, this sort of "art" merely calls itself that, but has jettisoned the essence of art: its aesthetic or artistic quality. Contemporary art practices, including various non-artistic experiments with classic art, can be called anything but art in its classic interpretation that is laid out in this essay. In any case, one thing is certain: they contain, in themselves, no spiritual-aesthetic potential (or, at most, merely primitive elements or simulacra of spirituality) that could satisfy the spiritual cravings of the postsecular person. Art practices and artifacts that currently fill contemporary museums and exhibition spaces, as well as so-called "performances" that crowd stages of theaters and concert halls, rather cater to the needs of the person of the secular age, which are devoid of any kind of spirituality. As a whole, they, as it were, foreshadow some sort of a spiritual—if not total—catastrophe that awaits humanity.[8] To be sure, all these artifacts and performances can arouse wonder and amazement, too, but only of a negative kind.

At the same time, postsecular people are not prone to apocalypticism. They have faith in life, in its spiritual foundations, in humanistic ideals, and in the ability of human rationality to go beyond its human boundaries. And aesthetic experience—provided one calls on it—can effectively assist them with this attitude.

Funding: This research received no external funding.

Conflicts of Interest: The author declares no conflict of interest.

References

Belyi, Andrei. 1994. *Kritika. Estetika. Teoriia simvolisma (Criticism. Aesthetics. Theory of Symbolism)*. Moscow: Iskusstvo, vol. 2.

Bennett, Jane. 2001. *The Enchantment of Modern Life: Attachments, Crossings, and Ethics*. Princeton: Princeton UP.

Berdyaev, Nikolai. 1985. *Sobranie sochinenii (Collected Works)*. Paris: YMCA, vol. 2.

Bychkov, Victor. 2007. *Russkaia Teurgicheskaia Estetika (Russian Theurgic Aesthetics)*. Moscow: Ladomir.

Bychkov, Victor. 2008. *Khudozhestvennyi Apokalipsis kul'tury (The Artistic Apocalypse of Culture)*. Moscow: Kul'turnaia Revoliutsiia, vol. 2.

Costa, Paolo. 2011. A Secular Wonder. In *The Joy of Secularism. 11 Essays for How We Live Now*. Edited by George Levine. Princeton: Princeton University Press, pp. 134–54.

Habermas, Jürgen. 2006. Religion in the Public Sphere. *European Journal of Philosophy* 14.1: 1–25. [CrossRef]

Ivanov, Vyacheslav. 1974. *Sobranie sochinenii (Collected Works)*. Brussels: Foyer Oriental Chrétien, vol. 2.

Kurtz, Paul, ed. 2000. *Humanist Manifesto 2000: A Call for a New Planetary Humanism*. Amherst: Prometheus Books.

---

[8] I examine this subject in my foundational study: Bychkov 2008.

Levine, George. 2006. *Darwin Loves You: Natural Selection and the Reenchantment of the World*. Princeton: Princeton University Press.

Mankovskaya, Nadya. 2016a. Esteticheskoe kredo 'demona' frantsuzskogo simvolizma Zhozefena Peladana. (The Aesthetic Creed of Joséphin Péladan, the 'Demon' of French Symbolism). *Voprosy Filosofii* 5: 80–92.

Mankovskaya, Nadya. 2016b. *Fenomen postmodernizma. Khudozhestvenno-esteticheskii rakurs (The Phenomenon of Postmodernism: An Artistic-Aesthetic Angle)*. St. Petersburg: Rossiiskie Propilei.

Péladan, Joséphin. 1898. *La Décadance Esthétique. Réponse à Tolstoï*. Paris: Chamuel.

Péladan, Joséphin. 1905. *Origine et Esthétique de la Tragédie*. Paris: Sansot.

Soloviev, Vladimir. 1966. *Sobranie Sochinenii (Collected Works)*. Brussels: Foyer Oriental Chrétien, vol. 1.

Taylor, Charles. 2011. Disenchantment-Reenchantment. In *The Joy of Secularism: 11 Essays for How We Live Now*. Edited by George Levine. Princeton: Princeton UP, pp. 57–73.

Vasalou, Sophia. 2015. *Wonder: A Grammar*. Albany: SUNY Press.

Warner, Michael, Jonathan Van Antwerpen, and Craig Calhoun, eds. 2010. *Varieties of Secularism in a Secular Age*. Cambridge: Harvard UP.

Welsch, Wolfgang. 1996. *Grenzgänge der Ästhetik*. Stuttgart: Philipp Reclam jun.

Willmott, Glenn. 2018. *Reading for Wonder: Ecology, Ethics, Enchantments*. Basingstoke: Palgrave Macmillan.

MDPI

St. Alban-Anlage 66

4052 Basel

Switzerland

Tel. +41 61 683 77 34

Fax +41 61 302 89 18

www.mdpi.com

Religions Editorial Office

E-mail: religions@mdpi.com

www.mdpi.com/journal/religions

www.ingramcontent.com/pod-product-compliance
Lightning Source LLC
Chambersburg PA
CBHW041146120626
46547CB00020B/3133